MW00638541

DISRUPT
——— Your ———
NOW

THE SUCCESSFUL ENTREPRENEUR'S GUIDE
TO REIMAGINING YOUR BUSINESS & LIFE

LISA KIPPS-BROWN

Disrupt Your Now: The Successful Entrepreneur's Guide to Reimagining Your Business & Life

Copyright © 2021 by Lisa Kipps-Brown lisakippsbrown.com

For information about special discounts for bulk purchases or booking Lisa Kipps-Brown for keynotes, training programs or workshops, both online and in-person, please contact info@lisakippsbrown.com.

Disclaimer:
This book contains the ideas and opinions of the author and other entrepreneurs with the intention of providing information and motivation to readers. The advice and strategies found within may not be suitable for every situation. Although every precaution has been taken to verify the accuracy of the information contained, the author and publisher assume no responsibility for errors, omissions, or results accrued from the advice in this book. The author and publisher urge readers to seek appropriate expert advice and legal counsel.

Also by Lisa Kipps-Brown:
Boomer Cashout: Increase Your Business's Value & Marketability to Sell for Retirement

First Paperback Edition July 2021
Published by Dragon's Tooth Publishing
Edited by Virginia L. Kipps

Kipps-Brown, Lisa
Disrupt Your Now: The Successful Entrepreneur's Guide to Reimagining Your Business & Life
ISBN: 978-1-7375008-0-3

For Wick and Ernern

You are my life.

Table of Contents

Foreword by Steve Sims..i

Acknowledgements...ii

Introduction..iii

How To Use This Book...vii

PART ONE: Getting "You" Right.......................................1

Chapter 1: It's Your Business and You Can Make It Anything You Want...1

You have to be brutally honest with yourself....................4

Sometimes you need to be challenged from the outside.....5

Are you in a fur-lined mousetrap?....................................7

Live life by design, not by default....................................9

Start each day with a clean slate!....................................12

The 4 pillars of happiness...13

Chapter 2: If a blind man can mow the grass, you can do this...17

Success doesn't require a 5-step plan...............................19

Become a spinmaster at turning negatives into positives. 22

"I was never trapped in prison; my mind was free"..........23

See reasons, not excuses..25

Sometimes inspiration lies within hardships....................28

Don't accept what others view as your destiny................30

Chapter 3: What's your victory condition?......................33

Starting with the "don't want's" can be easier.................34

Creating a lifestyle vs. focusing on growth.....................37

Don't Grow Just to Grow..40

Understand what motivates you..41

Concentrate on ROE and ROS...43

Living your best life..44

A nudge can be more powerful than a big change...........47

What's your definition of success? BUILD THAT..........49

Chapter 4: There's only one YOU......................................53

"I've been preparing for this my whole life"...................55

Are you a voice or an echo?..57

Being a night person isn't morally inferior......................60

Your shortcomings are your strengths..............................61

"It's like making lawn art"..64

"I'm so thankful I was born blind"...................................66

PART TWO - Expanding Your Network & Mind...........69

Chapter 5: Get in the right sandbox.................................69

Don't let your education limit you....................................71

Shatter your own glass ceiling..73

What's your canary in the coal mine?...............................75

There's gotta be a pony in this pile of doodoo.................76

It's okay to say no...78

Chapter 6: Create your own luck.....................................81

One business's junk is another business's gold mine.......84

Look for signs on the long and winding road...................86

The right mindset leads to the right opportunities 89

Moments that seem random can transform your life........90

Chapter 7: "The best thing I ever did was go to Elaine's."
...95

Surround yourself with the right people...........................97

You have to have people who push you............................98

Mentors provide shortcuts..101

You're never too small to have a procurement expert....103

Chapter 8: To get the right answers you have to ask the
right questions..107

"I'm a suit and tie guy"...109

Know who wants what you have.....................................111

There's power in choice...113

From never working to CEO...114

Buying a camera just makes you a camera owner..........116

PART THREE - Thinking & Creating............................119

Chapter 9: Focus on the customer's pain.........................119

Collaborate to promote change.......................................121

The magic & mystique of scarcity...................................123

Put on your 3D glasses..125

Winning the race to zero...126

Rethink the traditional..128

Treat your ideas like the original art they are.................131

Chapter 10: "No, bro, we just read the email you got."..133

Specialize to narrow the field...135

Develop a niche that both you and your clients love......137

"The author wins every time"...140

What's your polarizing brand trait?................................143

Chapter 11: Identifying the dragon...............................147

Adapt existing products to meet new markets...............149

"Fun, nothing, this is a business model" 151

Control and love your customer.....................................152

Solve your own problem...154

Or, get close to a problem you want to solve.................156

Start with something ugly and cheap..............................158

PART FOUR - Starting & Doing......................................163

Chapter 12: Focus your efforts on things that support your long term goals...163

Work on your business instead of in it............................165

Don't build your business on someone else's................167

Do what you're good at and delegate the rest.................170

Envision what you want and plan backwards.................171

Results are a reflection of process..................................174

Chapter 13: Get off your big BUT....................................177

Don't be a crab on the beach...178

Follow your dreams..180

Diversifying is a lifeline..183

Perfection means you never took off..............................186

Fuel growth through strategic 3-way wins.....................189

Chapter 14: What's the worst that could happen?..........193

Embrace your trauma to unleash your potential.............195

The one thing fear and faith have in common................198

The transformative effect of believing in yourself.........200

What are you waiting for?...202

Chapter 15: Giving up is the guaranteed route to failure.
....**205**

The sharks aren't always right..207

Obliterating boundaries..210

"If I can close Netflix on my own, why do I need to work
for someone else?"..212

"No" isn't forever...214

"There has to be a reason I'm still here".........................216

PART FIVE - Higher Purpose...221

Chapter 16: How many people will be at your funeral?. 221

Helping others helps your bottom line...........................222

"I have the whole prison system on my back"................224

"It's not my money"...225

Disruptive Philanthropy...227

102 Lessons From Lisa...231

Afterword by Charles Kipps...245

Appendix: Meet the Entrepreneurs..................................247

About the Author..253

Foreword by Steve Sims

As I started to write this foreword, it occurred to me that anybody who knows me knows I get straight to the point. While I could give you lots of impressive insights, I'll just be me and keep it simple.

Lisa's one of those weirdos like me that just thinks differently. She wrote *Disrupt Your Now* to help you get back to why you started your business in the first place: to live the life you want.

This is your chance to take a shortcut to getting a PhD in Life by learning from 50 successful entrepreneurs, many that I know personally. They've already been where you are, have already made the mistakes and are now enjoying the rewards, so why not learn from them?

Just read the damn book. And, while you're at it, maybe even have an old fashioned.

Steve D. Sims
Los Angeles, California
Author, *Bluefishing: The Art of Making Things Happen*

Acknowledgements

Kimley Blanks, I can't overstate my gratitude for your help staying focused and for herding me when necessary.

Steve Sims, thanks for making me do the things you know I need to do and for being so inspiring.

Charles and Ginger Kipps, thanks for all of your help and encouragement. I'm proud to have such talented cousins.

Ryan Garrett, thanks for your friendship and support. I'm so thankful Colin's racing brought us together to share half a brain.

Jeff Reed, thanks for connecting me with such great people, always believing in me, and being a true friend.

Dr. Hoby Wedler, thank you for just being you and for helping me remember how amazing Daddy was. I wish he could have known you.

A special thanks to all of the entrepreneurs who shared their time and experience to help me help others.

Most of all, thanks to Tom for all the years of love.

Introduction

2011 was the beginning of me almost losing my business and mind.

To set the stage, I need to backtrack a little to a comment I'd made to my husband Tom a few months earlier: "I've spent my entire life putting myself last. Now it's MY time. I'm gonna concentrate on myself and my business and build something really cool that I can sell for retirement!"

Piece of cake. I've got this – yeehah! My runway was wide open and I was soooo excited. The world was my oyster. I'd been an entrepreneurial idea factory for the past 20 years, anyway, so all I needed to do was figure out which of my ideas I wanted to run with.

Our kids were now adults and out on their own, healthy and happy. And I had a history of doing anything I set my mind to:

I'd sold two other businesses in the 90's, one that I started when the kids were just 4 months and 24 months old. I'd started my web and marketing strategy business in 1996 while raising them and cared for my father-in-law with Alzheimer's for over 7 years in our home. I'd taught myself how to develop a shopping cart in '97 from books I bought at now-defunct bookstores (in case you're too young to know, there was no Google yet and

Altavista couldn't index nonexistent information). I'd homeschooled the kids for a couple of years, moved the business and family to another state, volunteered innumerable hours, and served on multiple Boards.... What could possibly stop me from achieving this new goal?

Fast forward two weeks to a phone call from my mother: "I passed out while visiting a friend in assisted living and I'm afraid to drive home. Can you come and get me?"

Little did I know that this was the precursor to my creating a huge clusterf*** instead of something exciting I could sell. I won't go into the details of all that happened along the way, but the troubling signs I had noticed in Mama over the past several years were to be diagnosed as Alzheimer's later that year. In my heart I'd seen it coming because of the years I'd already lived under the same roof with that damn disease. Now it was entering my life again. I knew that the blackberry cobbler with the soupy middle, the phone calls to tell me something exciting that I had just called to tell her 10 minutes earlier, and the changes in her personality were all bad signs, but they were signs I was hoping I was wrong about. After all, she was the one who always kept me straight by reminding me of dates and times of events. How could she have Alzheimer's?

Alzheimer's itself is just the catalyst to what led to the

misery and chaos I created, though. In a nutshell, rather than doing for myself what I'd already spent 16 years doing for clients – helping them use technology to adapt their business to make or meet disruptive changes in their industry or personal life – I made a poor hiring decision that culminated in me spending the last 6 months of Mama's life working my ass off to save the business from potential bankruptcy, going into debt, hurting my staff, and hurting my family.

At this major crossroads in life I had turned in front of oncoming traffic and almost destroyed myself, my family, and my business. Tom had retired to help me care for Mama; if not for him, this whole thing would have been much worse and I doubt the business would exist now.

If that's not bad enough, that poor decision was the gift that just wouldn't quit giving. It left me with overwhelming guilt for the damage to my family. I was doubting myself professionally for the first time in my adult life, thinking of myself as a loser, afraid to trust my judgement any more, and seriously considering getting a job.

Anyone who knows me well knows that even considering getting a job is a serious sign of bad things going on in my mind. That would be the last thing this nonconformist would do!

Thankfully I, my family, and my business have survived but the episode has haunted me. I know there's a huge number of other entrepreneurs out there who are outwardly very successful but on the inside are miserable. They've built a business that isn't personally fulfilling, or they may be facing a life situation that has them on the verge of taking that figurative turn into oncoming traffic that I made.

While my own downward spiral began due to a major life transition, it doesn't really matter what has brought you to this point. What matters is that you take back your business, your life, your family, and yourself. If I can overcome the depths of despair I faced you can, too.

I've met so many amazing entrepreneurs in the process of rebuilding myself over the past several years, and many have been kind enough to share their personal experiences to help you. From internationally known experts to a convicted felon who spent 15 years in prison to a teen business owner, they're giving you the chance to take a shortcut by learning from their mistakes and successes.

I thank them all from the bottom of my heart and hope that you will, too, after reading this book.

How To Use This Book

Disrupt Your Now isn't meant to be a prescription. In fact, you're missing the entire point if you try to use it like that. And, if some things seem contradictory, that's because different things work for different people.

It's meant to spur you, maybe for the first time, to be honest with yourself about what you want out of life and figure out how your business can help you get it. Learning from the mistakes and successes of others can give you a shortcut, but just because something worked for them doesn't mean it's right for you. It's YOUR business and should help YOU get what YOU want. Other successful entrepreneurs are after what THEY want.

There are 3 basic business problems: how to make money, save money, and save time. Be careful, though, because you can create problems in one area in trying to solve for another. When caring for my mother, I was worried about the business continuing without me working as much so I hired. With the increased pressure for cash flow and fallout from hiring the wrong person, I ended up working more than I ever had and going into debt. I was worse off in both time and money, with stress through the roof, the exact opposite of what I wanted to achieve! I should have cut services and fired clients. That would have been so simple.

The same decisions can never meet every entrepreneur's needs, though, even in the same industry. Think about just a few of the things that different people may want or value differently:

- Whether you have employees and how many;
- How much daily work is required on your part;
- The ability to create residual or passive income;
- Having freedom of time or location;
- Not having to do the same type of work every day;
- Creating a product or service that can be sold to a larger company;
- Building a business you can sell or one you can just walk away from if the mood strikes.

Having said that, it's time to get your brain going so you can disrupt your own now! The Appendix at the end of the book has a list of all entrepreneurs featured in the book, and a link to more information about them. Some of the chapters also include links to videos and other content.

If you feel like you need more structure, there's also the *Disrupt Your Now Companion Guide* to help you work through your thoughts (lisakippsbrown.com/dyn-guide).

You can reach out to me at lisakippsbrown.com/contact or book a free consult at lisakippsbrown.com/free-consult if you need help. Good luck on your journey!

PART ONE: Getting "You" Right

Chapter 1

It's your business and you can make it anything you want.

Do you remember why you started your business in the first place?

If you're like most entrepreneurs, it's probably some combination of wanting to be your own boss, be in control of your income level and how much you work, and make a living doing what you love with clients or customers you like.

You probably had a very clear vision of what you imagined your future would be like, even if you didn't really know how you'd get there. Whether your dream dinner was in an exclusive restaurant or by a campfire, you had your own unique view of what success would mean and feel like to you.

The problem is, there's a good chance you've built something that now has you feeling trapped, frustrated, broke, miserable, or maybe even scared.

You probably got to where you are by building your business like everyone else in your industry, unfortunately forgetting that it's YOUR business. Fear that you'll be left behind, left out, or overlooked if you don't follow the trends in your industry or offer all the services and products your competitors do is a great way to build the business you never wanted to own.

I get it. I've been there, too.

One day I looked in the mirror, though, and told myself, "It's your business and you can make it anything you want. Why are you making the choices you are?"

Continually reminding myself of that was the beginning of my turnaround and can be the beginning of yours, too.

The good news is that it's never too late to make a change! It could be small changes that add up to big differences or even a huge shift in direction. Everyone's journey is different and the changes one person makes aren't the changes another should make.

Do me a favor: take a few minutes, transport yourself back to when you first started your business, and think about these questions:

- Why did you want to start a business?
- What were your dreams and passions?
- What types of things did you envision yourself doing in the business?

- How did you envision your work schedule?
- What were you feeling and thinking?
- What was the future you imagined?

Now fast forward back to the present.

- Is the business anything like you thought it could be?
- If not, were your dreams unrealistic or did you get off track?
- What are your favorite things to do or sell, and what things do you despise?
- What's the most profitable service or item you sell?
- Is it one of the things you like or one that you hate?
- Can you make a living going with only your favorites?
- What would happen if you just ditched the stuff you hate?

Only when you know what you really want and why you want it can you get it. Knowing why is just as important as knowing what because why puts it in the hierarchy of needs. The more important something is to you personally, the less negotiable it should be in your life.

LESSON: Remembering your dreams is the beginning of reimagining your business to reinvent your life.

You have to be brutally honest with yourself

We entrepreneurs are a strange lot. We tend to have big egos and don't look at our own ideas as critically as we should. After all, our ideas are so awesome they have to be successful, right? Anyone who can't see that is unworthy of our time. They need to stick their head back in the sand.

The problem is, we're usually too close to the forest to see the trees.

If you're serious about making changes, it's time to do whatever it takes to look at the big picture as objectively as possible. It's the only way you'll be able to identify changes you can make to improve your business and life.

You may be able to do it on your own, but I'm willing to bet that you'll need someone from the outside who can be truly objective and ask you the right questions to help uncover the truth.

I strongly encourage you to start thinking about people you can reach out to for help in charting your course. Just don't ask a family member or close friend, though, because they'll have a harder time being objective and you may also react too emotionally to their advice (or criticism!). Often friends and family are afraid for you to take the risk, or afraid you'll outgrow them and they'll be left behind.

Whether it's a coach, mastermind, mentor, therapist, or some combination, depends on your situation and personality. Whoever it is, though, you need advice from people who have been where you are and can relate to what you're going through. If you're not sure what you need, you can schedule a free call with me at lisakippsbrown.com/free-consult.

> **LESSON:** If you're too proud to be honest with yourself, you may as well stop reading now.

Sometimes you need to be challenged from the outside

Steve Sims, author of the international bestseller *Bluefishing: The Art of Making Things Happen* accidentally started his luxury concierge business, but what an accident that was! With clients like Sir Richard Branson, Elon Musk, and Sir Elton John, Steve had it made. You know – the house, the motorcycles, the spectacular events in Monaco, Palm Beach, and Macau. The glitz and glamour. The billionaires lining up for him to help them check something amazing off their bucket list and create a great brag story. Pretty good for a kid who grew up in East London and quit school at 15, huh?

A funny thing happened, though. People kept saying he should write a book about how he built the business. Figuring it was an interesting challenge (and you know how we entrepreneurs love a good challenge), he managed to get picked up by a major publishing house, got a great advance, and wrote the book. Truth is, though, he didn't think much past that and didn't even plan a launch party.

If he could have foreseen the transformative effect that book would have on his life, I guarantee you he'd have thrown one hell of a launch party!

Suddenly the accidental entrepreneur had an accidental international bestseller that thrust him onto the world stage, moving from exclusive rooms with the mega wealthy to having thousands of entrepreneurs from all over the world and across all industries clamoring for his advice, including me.

Although he already had a wildly successful company, the outside challenge of writing the book is what made Steve realize that the natural talents and assets he had used to build that company in the hospitality and travel industry could transcend industries. He realized that "realtors and Cartier have the same problems." Without having the amazing response to the book to open his mind, he may have never realized that his talents are portable.

Steve has transformed his life from being paid huge sums to create bragging stories for the wealthy to being paid to truly change people's lives. That's something he never would have imagined, and it's so much more fulfilling.

Steve says "I'm a lot happier now, I'm a lot smilier now. I really enjoy my new life and it's done so much more for our family. I could never conceive!"

> **LESSON:** Pay attention to what other people are suggesting you do. They often see things in you and recognize opportunities that you don't.

Are you in a fur-lined mousetrap?

The first time I heard that term was when I was fresh out of college and working in the Controller's area for a global manufacturer. I understood what it meant but couldn't imagine ever being in that situation. How could someone ever be willing to give up their happiness, identity, and dreams by not being brave enough to break free from a job they felt trapped in?

As I matured and got married, bought a house, had kids, and started businesses, of course I could then understand why someone could be in that situation. I'm blessed in that I've never been a "keeping up with the Joneses" type of person, which makes it a lot easier for me to avoid that fur-lined mousetrap. Truthfully, though, I'm kind of weird in that way.

Most people value the ability to live in the right neighborhoods, drive the right cars, wear the right brands and jewelry, belong to the right clubs, take the right vacations, own the right toys, and send their kids to the right schools. There's nothing wrong with that! When it's a problem is when it causes you to sacrifice other things you value in order to maintain that fur-lined mousetrap.

Things like time with your family, doing work you love with clients you actually like, relaxing on weekends, taking fun vacations, and just enjoying life before it's too late.

If you now find yourself in that mousetrap, it's time to make some hard decisions about what you're willing to sacrifice materially and in perceived status. Would you rather be happy or impress people with material things?

You may not need to sacrifice materially, though. It may be that you just need to change the way you work, the type of work you do, the rates you charge, and the clients you accept. I had a client who was working almost every night on proposals, quotes, and invoicing. Just getting them set up on a client relationship management system that automated much of the work ended up saving them about 20 hours every week, and also made their customers happier!

You may have trouble grasping that there are some people who just don't deserve to work with you. I know you need cash flow, but at what expense? After going through their client list with another of my clients, we found they were actually losing money by working with a client they thought they couldn't do without. On top of that, the client acted like a prima donna and demanded priority attention. The opportunity cost of giving priority attention to a client who's a net loss makes your loss even bigger and your days more miserable. Ditch them.

> **LESSON:** Now is the time to decide the things that are most important to you and what you're willing to change to get them.

Live life by design, not by default

Psychiatrist Manuel Astruc's twin sister had died of cancer one month earlier and the photo he was looking at hit him like a hammer. Already battling cancer, Magdalena was smiling and happy.

It was striking to him that she had handled her illness and all that life handed her so well, and he had everything but was miserable. In that watershed moment, he literally made a commitment to change his attitude and habits and learn to enjoy the ride. Couldn't he at least do that in honor of her life that was cut short?

Until that moment, he had "lived life by default instead of by design." His parents had an expectation that he would become a doctor, so he did. He learned to work hard, thinking that all his problems could be solved by working harder but eventually realized that "you can't just keep working harder."

He was moving too little and had a horrible diet but that was about to end.

Manuel says, "This was my line in the sand, the moment of truth: I have to start enjoying things." He immediately put up blinders to all the negativity that he was wallowing in. He made a conscious decision to ignore negative thoughts and started looking forward.

In putting up those blinders, he removed everything he possibly could that had been contributing to negativity in his life. He turned off the news, where the 24-hour cycle is driven by negative stories. The drive to work had always been spent listening to sports radio but now he realized "they had stopped talking about excellence and started talking about drama." Gone was sports radio and in its place he started listening to audiobooks and podcasts, things that inspired him. He began to feel that he had a "tribe of virtual mentors." He no longer felt alone.

He also focused on moving more: rather than beginning an ambitious workout plan, he decided to "do something small every single day." It's no surprise that the more he did, the more he felt like doing. If he had started out trying to do too much, though, he may have faltered.

Next he began to change his diet, once again small steps at a time, changing one meal a day starting with breakfast. Past breakfasts void of nutrients were replaced with healthy smoothies. After having a healthy breakfast became a habit, he moved to lunch.

The changes he made – putting up blinders to negativity, moving more, and eating better – fed him holistically in three ways: through meals, energy, and knowledge.

He began to create "intentional enjoyment" throughout his day. He says, "that doesn't mean everything grinds to a halt; it can be part of your normal work day." It can be as simple as realizing how nice the warm sun feels on your face or listening to a song you like.

You don't need to follow a militant regimen to improve your life; just focusing on enjoying small things has a compound effect on improving your attitude.

Manuel had put himself on a drip feed of positivity, making it harder for anything negative to break through. He says he had found a way to "soften the sharp, critical voice that high performers have." He was finally giving himself the grace he gives others.

For the first time in many years, Manuel fully realized that "there's hope, change is possible, and you don't have to be alone." He began to make it his mission to help other high achievers learn how to be happy and satisfied, and says, "the payoff is that I've been having fun."

> **LESSON:** Small changes can add up to truly living your life by design.

Start each day with a clean slate!

Everyone has their own ways of setting goals and motivating themselves but I just love this one:

Richard Mulholland, founder of the presentation powerhouse Missing Link and author of the books *Legacide*, *Boredom Slayer*, and *Story Seller*, doesn't believe in New Year's resolutions. Instead, he begins each day with a New Day Resolution. At the end of the day he gives himself a victory emoji if he achieves the day's resolution and a poop emoji if he doesn't. Then he also awards himself by the week, month, and year, making the positive effect cumulative.

Rich says, "the most important detail for me is that I only need five ✌ a week for my week to be a ✌ and only three ✌ for my month to be a 🏆, and then only eleven 🏆 for my year to be a 🔥. The critical detail is that failure is not final. This keeps me going, and a broken streak doesn't reset the clock – which is why I think New Year's Resolutions fail."

Rich has gamified his goals, making them more fun to track and more motivating to meet; it also feeds into what he says about your "victory condition" in Chapter 3. Recognizing what you've achieved always feels great but looking at a poop emoji doesn't feel nearly as bad as the awful self-talk most of us do when we don't do something we planned to do. ✌ or 💩 – it's quick, easy, no grey areas, and the smiling poop cheers you on for another day even if you didn't get it done today.

It's so much easier to do something big when we break it down into chunks, and creating achievable New Day Resolutions can be key to reaching the goals you've been dreaming of.

I've found that a New Day Resolution also gives me a more positive mindset than a to-do, plus a resolution can be to NOT do something, like not doing work that you should be delegating. Can you imagine how much more time you'd have to pursue your dream life if you reached that resolution on a regular daily basis? It's kind of hard to put a "don't do" on a to-do list.

> **LESSON:** Figure out a way to encourage yourself to do something every day, even if it seems tiny, to help you reach your goals.

The 4 pillars of happiness

As Manuel Astruc so eloquently puts it, "when you have the gift of desperation people are hungry to learn. The alternative sucks."

As part of his own transformation, he created a coaching business to help successful entrepreneurs manage burnout. We all know that money by itself doesn't buy happiness, and sometimes the most financially successful of us are the most miserable. The personality types that make successful entrepreneurs often aren't open to changes we need to make, though.

Through his research, Manuel has created what he calls the "4 Pillars of Happiness." I think they provide a framework that all of us can relate to and learn from:

1. **We're never-finished products.** We need to continue to grow and learn, and not just in ways that make us more money. It's important to nurture your personal growth as well as you nurture your business growth.

2. **Connections and community are huge.** You may not want to admit you need others, but you do. Whether you're enjoying something recreational or sharing ideas, it's well documented that those who have strong connections with family, friends, and colleagues are more likely to be happy, healthy, and successful. You can't do it alone.

3. **Blaze your own trail.** If you understand yourself, your passions, your strengths, and your values, you're more likely to find what you're truly meant to do. This leads to more fulfillment and less chance of burnout and being swayed by others' opinions.

4. **Commit to enjoy the ride, no matter what.** Manuel has learned through his own life that being happy is a choice. We can choose to focus on the negative and unhealthy, or we can choose to focus on the positive, healthy, and re-energizing. Some people just naturally look for

the good in everything, and you can train yourself to do the same.

In our conversation Manuel reminded me of what Viktor Frankel wrote in *Man's Search For Meaning*, "Everything can be taken from a man but one thing: the last of the human freedoms – to choose one's attitude in any given set of circumstances, to choose one's own way."

Often it's hard to recognize what you can and can't control when you're mired in the middle of it, though. That's when you might need some outside help just to help you recognize the difference.

A B2B client was constantly complaining about the sales staff that his own clients hired. They were a pain for him to have to deal with, for sure, but he wasted a ton of energy just bitching about them. The staff and company were oblivious, though, so it was only hurting him. I recommended that he offer a free session to help train them and told him to pitch it as a way to help staff increase their income. That would make it be viewed positively rather than negatively.

After the engaging training presentation, their staff was energized and more knowledgeable so sales did indeed increase. Just as importantly, end customer complaints and returns decreased. The company actually started asking for his input in hiring new staff, too. He turned his problem into a solution for his client that helped him and everyone else – and made him more valuable to his client. The alternative would have been to just continue bitching and nothing would have changed.

> **LESSON:** Concentrate on what you can control rather than worry about what you can't control.

Chapter 2

Now it's time to start checking your confidence and mindset...

My father was blind and I literally never remember him saying he couldn't do something because of being blind. He NEVER used it as an excuse.

When my new best friend in high school started hanging out at our house I didn't think to tell her that he was blind. After she'd been coming to our house for a couple of months someone at school mentioned he was blind. She said, "no, he's not!" And I had to say "yes, he is!" She was dumbfounded and still swears she saw him driving his company truck down Main Street. I believe her.

He owned a music store, rode horses, shot guns, played HORSE and Around the World basketball games with us, and used a lathe in the woodworking shop he set up in our basement. I even found out years after he died of leukemia that he piloted a boat for his sighted friends to waterski! I'm sure there was somebody beside him at the helm, but still...

So how does mowing the grass fit in? Before my sisters and I were old enough to do it, he mowed while barefoot, using his highly developed sense of touch to tell which grass was mowed and which wasn't. I can assure you there were no strips of missed grass in our yard! He was a perfectionist.

We're all guilty of making excuses for why we haven't done something but I'm serious when I say I never heard him use his blindness as an excuse. Sure, we had to do things like read him the dates on the coins he collected but here are just a few of the things I remember him doing. They're things that we took for granted because he was just Daddy, but the vast majority of men I know *who can see* have never done most of them:

- built a horse trailer that was registered and legal for use on the highway;
- made a wooden lamp for me that was shaped like an oil lamp;
- finished out two bedrooms in our basement, sheetrock and all;
- changed the tires on Mama's car;
- trained our pony to sit down and roll over;
- built a house with a tall, peaked roof for our pet goat (yes, we had a menagerie);
- grew and harvested grapes, and then made wine from them;
- told me to stop sticking my tongue out at him –

hahaha. Now that did freak me out. My sisters and I spent lots of time after that trying to figure out if he'd been tricking us about being blind.

The point is, it's time for you to decide whether you're going to do something or just talk about doing something. It's easy to talk about it, but actually doing it takes time, effort, and strength of character. It takes work. You have to be willing to look foolish and also to fail – that's all part of the process.

If you want security and low risk, get a job. Otherwise, get cracking and start working on your attitude!

> **LESSON:** Stop using convenient excuses for not doing the things you're capable of; free your mind and the rest will follow.

Success doesn't require a 5-step plan

So many entrepreneur books include what are basically prescriptions: do these things in this order and you'll succeed. The problem is, everyone is made differently and what works for one doesn't for another.

A few months ago I read a bestseller that had great advice overall. BUT. Then it included a "do this" prescription, not as in "this is what worked for me" but as in "if you do this you'll find the same success as I did."

I'm old enough to know better, old enough to pick out

what resonates with me and my personality and ditch the rest, but for some reason this time I decided "I can do this." Dumb move. I went to bed that night all pumped to start following it the next morning and then my brain rebelled. Just the thought of following that prescription put me into a spiral for a week even though I never actually started trying to follow it!

Aside: I also realized later that even thinking about following it was a way to procrastinate on something else I was supposed to be thinking about. Kind of like when I installed Windows 98 just after its initial launch, when I was in the middle of writing a book and it crashed my computer. I *never* upgrade anything until the early bugs are worked out, yet I chose to do this major upgrade right in the middle of writing a book. Major self-sabotage, Einstein...

B. Jeffrey Madoff knows himself well and makes no apologies for what he's like, though. He says, "if you're looking for someone who had a great plan and executed on that plan, it's not me. I can't do 5 action points. I have no plan in the morning."

Yet, he has decades of proven success building an apparel company fresh out of college and being named one of the Top 10 Young Designers in the US although he had no previous experience in the industry, and building Madoff Productions into the top-rated video production company in New York City. He has a few clients you may have heard of, like Ralph Lauren, Victoria's Secret, Gucci, Godiva, and Tiffany & Co.

He's also the author of *Creative Careers: Making a Living With Your Ideas*, and a playwright and theater producer.

According to Jeffrey, the one consistent thing in his life is that he's always been "seduced by ideas."

He started his apparel company straight out of college when a good friend asked what he could do to "earn more than bank interest." Jeffrey thought "well, I could do clothes," because he didn't know anything else to do. His friend invested and could he ever do clothes! His company more than doubled every couple of months.

Jeffrey says, "I was ignorant, but fortunately not stupid."

He fell in love with New York City while traveling there for his fashion business. Being "a stimulus junkie," he decided to move there. He made the transition into film after working with Dennis Hopper on developing a film project. Madoff was again, self-taught.

As a child, Jeffrey had created a movie theater in his basement, chose the films, and did the sound effects and music for them since they were silent. As an adult, he found himself doing much the same thing. It didn't take a 5-step plan for him to find his calling; he just followed his attraction to ideas.

In my case, I loved reading mysteries and solving puzzles growing up. In my business I enjoy things like researching how web technology can be used to solve a problem or troubleshooting to reverse engineer a bug. Even though I love working with people and brainstorming, I also like going into my cave every once in a while to work on something that doesn't require interacting with others. I know I need that downtime to recharge for working with people.

> **LESSON:** Pay attention to what you liked as a child; it may just hold the secret to your success and fulfillment as an adult.

Become a spinmaster at turning negatives into positives

We all have bad days. Those days when nothing seems to go right, the stars are aligned against us, and we just can't catch a break.

I was having one of those days when Tamara Linnan, hashtag queen, veteran, and founder of Profitable Shenanigans, messaged me on Facebook asking what's happening. I replied "my day is sucking."

Her reply:

"Nope, it's not sucking. It's behind schedule for being awesome. #onlyskittlesoverhere"

And just like that I was smiling!

"Behind schedule for being awesome" is a brilliant way to look at things that aren't going right. Instead of focusing on everything that's going wrong, flipping it to being "behind schedule" means you're still on the right track. You just need a bit more time to get there.

And who can't feel a little happier when you think of Skittles?

> **LESSON:** Make it a habit to consciously look for a positive way to look at anything negative. There's always a flipside.

"I was never trapped in prison; my mind was free"

Shawn Barksdale's father got addicted to drugs and ended up going to prison when Shawn was a little boy. He and his mother moved back to her childhood home in Halifax County, Virginia, the county I live in. Shawn was raised by his grandparents and great grandparents, who taught him how to love and nurture. He lived on a farm, learned a good work ethic, and had strong authority figures.

Sadly, his great grandfather passed away when Shawn was just 10 years old, leaving a void in his life. During adolescence he started getting in with the wrong crowd, "getting in trouble here and there. I had charisma, I was a good person and people liked me but I was doing knucklehead stuff."

It escalated, though, and at age 23 Shawn went to prison for almost 15 years for armed robbery. A week before he was sentenced he found out he was going to be a father. He was an only child whose father had gone to prison for drugs and now his child would be born with her father in prison.

He knew one thing clearly: he wanted to change his life, not just for himself but for his child.

Shawn says, "I knew what a goal was but I didn't know how to reach one. I remember sitting on my floor in my cell, and I just started writing goals out." Some of his first goals:

- I want to get my GED.
- I want to be a good father.
- I want to take college courses.
- I want to learn about business.

Asking himself *ok, well how are you gonna do it?*, his mental reply was *today, just today, I'm gonna work on going to school. I don't know about tomorrow but I'm gonna do it today*.

Shawn went that day, the next day, and the next day, and "the next thing I know a week has gone by, then a month, and the next thing I know I had a GED. That was a goal that was obtained and I was like *oh, wow! I can accomplish something and it doesn't have to be something bad!*"

Shawn says, "I had a base to get back to because of my great grandparents and grandparents. I knew, ok, I have manners, I have morale, I have these things that I just have to pull back into, and that's what I started doing. I lined myself back up."

"Even when you're in prison and you're working for 27 and 35 cents and 45 cents, I still made sure of the mindset, it's a mindset. I never was trapped in there – my mind was free. My body was there but I read so many books."

There's more to tell of Shawn's story later in the book, but you'll be happy to know that he's now an entrepreneur and community leader. And because his mother brought his daughter to visit him regularly, they were able to build and maintain a relationship. She's now a student at Virginia Commonwealth University where she's on the Dean's List.

LESSON: Mindset is everything.

See reasons, not excuses

Those who make a difference see reasons where everyone else sees excuses. There's probably never been a time in our lifetimes when this was more apparent than during the COVID shutdown.

Most people put everything on hold for this 100-year pandemic, afraid to do anything or make any kind of change until it was over. Too much risk! Too scary!

But then you have those who looked at this as a 100-year opportunity, a watershed time that created opportunities the likes of which would never be seen again.

Sande Golgart, President of Zonez, is in the business of designing and manufacturing modular privacy suites which ship flat, can be quickly installed, and can grow with a company. They're perfect for anything from private conversations to breastfeeding moms and are a great way for a company to convert space without construction costs.

When COVID hit, though, all of a sudden offices were closed. Nobody needed to order Zonez privacy suites if they weren't even open. The future looked grim since there was no way to know how long the shutdown would last. If Zonez wanted excuses, they didn't need to look far.

Rather than hunkering down and just trying to ride it out, though, Sande says "we decided to find out where companies needed to be met on the other side of the pandemic." They conducted a research campaign in April, just a month after the shutdown started, and found that two things would change forever: declassification of workspaces and air filtration.

Their engineers realized everyone would be thinking about making HVAC systems better able to clean air. The problem is, that still left potentially contaminated air that would have to be sucked across rooms and people who would breathe it in before it could be cleaned.

They realized the air needed to be blocked and filtered right at the point of exhalation. It seems so obvious, doesn't it?

The team brainstormed and were able to create their new Clean Zonez product in just one month! Their patent-pending technology physically blocks air between coworkers, so any air that's been exhaled, coughed, or sneezed is pulled into a 4-layer air filtration system that sterilizes it.

This amazing product even has a standalone desktop option that only weighs 5 pounds and can be carried wherever you go.

The next time you find yourself making an excuse for not doing something, try to think of a reason that the excuse makes you need to DO something else. For example, if you didn't work out because you didn't have time, use that as a reason to find ways to free up time.

> **LESSON:** Every problem creates an opportunity; flip the excuses for why you can't succeed into reasons that you must.

Sometimes inspiration lies within hardships

After graduating from high school in South Carolina, Sherman Williams was working three jobs just trying to pay rent. One of the jobs was as a janitor at a college, picking up trash after people who were getting an education. He said he was "always following the rule of law, but it seemed like the rule of law didn't apply the same to everyone. So I said, 'You know what? I have to find a way to make it apply and make a difference.' "

Knowing he needed to get away to find himself, he decided to join the Army. He always felt he was destined "to be something great. I just had to figure out what it was." The Army ended up being the perfect place for him to do that.

Serving in combat during Operation Iraqi Freedom, he experienced the harsh arid environment, extreme heat and cold of the desert, and sandstorms. He was shocked at the effects on his skin: during the heat of the day it would feel "like it would just want to crack and peel off of me." Then the cold would hit at night.

This experience made Sherman start researching water

and the body's need for it, the minerals and other nutrients required to support our skin (the body's largest organ), and the negative effects of caffeine, and artificial colors and flavors.

All of this resulted in him creating Body Aqua functional beverages, "the beverage with a purpose." His unique products are all diabetic and vegan friendly, and have no caffeine, coloring, or artificial flavorings. After years of research, product development, and overcoming hurdles to get funding, he's currently producing 4 different products that are sold in stores like Walmart, Costco, and online:

- Body Aqua Skin Support, the world's first "cosmetic beverage," contains nutrients specifically for the skin: zinc, vitamins A, B3, B5, C, and E, folic acid, copper, biotin, chromium, and niacin.

- Body Aqua Fitness Beverage, the first flavored beverage that naturally boosts metabolism without the use of caffeine, provides over 1000% daily value of key nutrients in each bottle, and combines B6, B12, Vitamin C, Choline, L-Thea nine and Niacin for appetite control and natural energy.

- Well Water, which replaces over 72 key ionic minerals that are stripped in modern filtration processes.

- Kids Aqua, containing no colors or sodium, is

low sugar and diabetic friendly, and is packed with vitamins especially for kids.

Sherman is also breaking ground in other ways: he's the first Black Owned, Service Disabled Veteran Owned sponsor in NASCAR, where he partners with driver Colin Garrett to combat the epidemic of veteran suicide (I'm the team's marketing strategist and you'll find out more in the last chapter). He's constantly giving back to the community that helped him figure out what he was meant to do and how he was going to reach the greatness he knew he was destined for.

> **LESSON:** Your toughest challenges can provide breakthroughs that change your life.

Don't accept what others view as your destiny

The common belief is that it's pretty much impossible for a convicted felon to get a job, and that's considered a reason for the high rate of recidivism. When I met Shawn Barksdale, I assumed he had become an entrepreneur because he couldn't find a job. Wrong.

As a matter of fact, at one point Shawn was working 3 jobs when he was first released! He had debt to pay and wanted to clear that out as soon as possible.

While incarcerated he had earned a Server® certification and his first job after being released was at Burger King.

Shawn says, "I worked at Burger King like I was working at a 5-star restaurant." That's called pride in your work. It's proving to others, both your employer and customers, that you care about yourself and about the company that is paying you.

He continues, "in 30 days I was opening and closing, and was doing so well they wanted me to manage another store." Turns out he didn't accept that position because he already had another job lined up to work in the printing industry.

A 20-year employee was retiring and the company was using a staffing agency to fill the position. The agency was blown away by the trade certifications Shawn was pulling out, having assumed they would have a hard time finding anyone with the experience the company was looking for.

There was one drawback: although he'd been offered the job, the hire date was uncertain because the employee hadn't set a specific retirement date yet. He had been hired much faster than the company had imagined they'd be able to find someone qualified.

Shawn continued working at Burger King while waiting, and said "even though I had a job lined up I acted like I didn't." At a time when most of us would have gotten complacent and seen that as a time to coast, he didn't take anything for granted and continued to give his job at

BK his all. If the printing job had fallen through, I'm sure that Burger King would have been happy for him to stay.

That new job actually ended up providing the opportunity for Shawn to fulfill his dream of being an entrepreneur, but you have to wait a bit for that story.

> **LESSON:** Conventional wisdom isn't set in stone. You can prove it wrong with the right work ethic and preparing yourself for opportunities that may arise.

Chapter 3

Do you even know what would make you feel like you're successful?

Richard Mulholland commented to me that many "entrepreneurs aren't happy because they don't know their 'enough.' Businesses don't have a natural victory condition like board games. The only condition is growth, growth, growth, growth. That's like cancer; that makes no sense."

Analogies really help clarify thoughts for me, and this observation is right on target. Imagine if you could create your own entrepreneurial board game that lets you create and adapt your business and victory condition as the game progresses.

Do you know what your own victory condition would be?

I challenge you to write down what your perfect life would look like and then look at your business through that lens. Is it helping you get closer to or further away from that perfect life? If further away, you might not need to make major changes. It may just take some "nudges" as you'll read about in a bit, and my 1-hour No Gobbledygook Brainstorm might be all you need to clarify things (lisakippsbrown.com/brainstorm).

> **LESSON:** If you don't know where you're going, you won't know when you get there.

Starting with the "don't want's" can be easier

It can be overwhelming to decide what you really want your life to look like. Henry Sims, co-owner of Sims Media, felt overwhelmed at the thought of trying to decide what he wanted because "I might not have ever seen it, so how could I know I want it?" He found it much easier to start with what he knew he didn't want.

Studying mechanical engineering for two years in Oregon, he enjoyed the course work but realized that the day-to-day work in internships wasn't what he thought it would be. Out went mechanical engineering. He also realized he didn't like the rain and cold so that nixed Oregon and he returned to Los Angeles.

As a kid he and his Dad, Steve Sims, had gone to an entrepreneur retreat for kids and parents. That was the first time Henry was ever asked what he wanted his life to look like and he "had not a clue." He was supposed to write it down and said, "I don't know, but I know I don't want this and this," so they told him to start there.

Now, as a young adult he knew he wanted freedom over his own time and physical location, and didn't want rain or cold. He also didn't want to be an entrepreneur because he had grown up as the kid of an entrepreneur and thought it was too stressful (you'll read more about why in Chapter 5). Since he wasn't sure about anything else, he went back to the advice from that retreat and decided to learn more about what he didn't want while he explored what he might want.

At that point he still thought he wanted a job, just in a different area of expertise, and he began to immerse himself in as many different things as he could to explore different lifestyles. Knowing the diversity of people who come to a Sims Speakeasy, he thought that would be a great place to talk with others to see what they're doing and how they're building their life.

We actually first met at Speakeasy Reno in 2019 and had a conversation about my having started my business in '96 for freedom over my life and schedule, and how I love being in an industry that's constantly evolving. I asked if he thought he wanted to be an entrepreneur and his answer was a firm no, because he'd had enough of that lifestyle, but he was still trying to figure out what he did want. I remember thinking to myself in Reno, *I bet he ends up being an entrepreneur*. Being around a group of people who are all creating the life they want, not what somebody else wants, and then going into a structured job would be really hard.

Aside from the Speakeasies, Henry jumped into as many business meetings as people would let him, "just to listen and see what they were doing, and as many masterminds as possible to see how other people lived."

Through all of that investigation, Henry began to realize that he did have the entrepreneurial spirit and that he just needed to structure a business in the way that creates the life he wants to live. After almost 2 years of self-discovery and starting his own digital marketing business for a while, he and Steve are now partners in a new company called Sims Media, where they're each able to apply their own unique talents in a way that comes together to improve life for their clients.

The fact that Steve had successfully shifted his own entrepreneurial journey over the past several years to an industry he's much happier in also helped Henry realize that he doesn't have to be stuck in one industry as an entrepreneur and life can be anything he wants it to be.

In my own journey, I couldn't have known I was interested in web development when I was studying accounting in college since the web as we know it didn't exist until 15 years later. When I started developing sites in 1995, I saw it as a way that I could combine my business, entrepreneurial, and creative interests into one thing that was much more fulfilling to me.

Over the years I've been fortunate to have been able to do things as varied as helping save companies from bankruptcy by diversifying using the web to tripling CARES Act money for rural communities by developing a matching gift card program. All the while, my own business has evolved as the web and my life stages have. Except for the consequences of the bad decisions I made while caring for my mother, I've been very fortunate to have had a great 25 years and no one year has been the same as another. I'm constantly learning, and that's the way I like it.

> **LESSON:** It can be much easier to know what you don't want than what you want, so start there in envisioning your life.
>
> **BONUS LESSON:** Even if you don't want something, it might just be because you haven't seen it in a form you would like yet.

Creating a lifestyle vs. focusing on growth

The Derek & Romaine show was on Sirius XM for over twelve years and, when it was cancelled, Derek Hartley and Romaine Patterson transitioned into a podcast (more about this in Chapter 8). Since he'd never started a business, Derek took the time to listen to a podcast for startups where he learned a valuable lesson. "There are basically two kinds of businesses you can start: one that you expect to grow and be worth millions of dollars one day, or one that you can create a life around."

Derek said, "Sometimes people feel like, *I'm starting a business so now I have to be in this space of having to get investors and I've gotta build or franchise out or whatever this thing is,"* but he realized it doesn't have to be like that. That's what enabled them to decide on the length of the podcast and the time of day they would do it.

At the network, he said, "it used to be four hours a day from 6 to 10 at night and we weren't able to go to dinner with anyone, we couldn't go to movies, we couldn't have a life. Romaine had a child at home and she wasn't able to be there to put her child to bed at night. So, we were dedicated to this job but we didn't control our hours. When we had control over our own hours we both said, *I don't wanna work until 10 or 11 at night. I want a show where we're done at a reasonable hour, where the listeners are commuters*. On satellite radio we needed to be on four hours at a time because you never knew when people were coming in and out. But the way our show is now, people can listen live or they can listen any time so we don't need to be on for four hours for people to reach us. We don't need to do more than an hour."

Thanks to the startup podcast he listened to, he realized before they even started the business that "we're building a lifestyle for ourselves and we have to find our own parameters. How hard we want to work, how many hours we want to work, and what our priorities are in life. Ultimately, we have a good life. I think for any business owner, being able at the end of the day to have a level of satisfaction saying *you know what? I put in an honest day's work, I'm not stressed out, this is solid, I'm happy with what I'm doing, I'm within my own comfort zone of what I want to accomplish and what I want to achieve and I feel good about what I've built*. For anyone who owns a business, that's all you can ask for in a business and we've been so lucky that we have a core audience that has been so supportive of us."

The point Derek makes dovetails with my earlier point: it's your business and you can make it anything you want. If you want to grow a large business that's great. But if you want a business you can build a life around you'll need to make totally different types of decisions. Don't make the mistake of modeling your business around one whose owner didn't have the same priorities as yours. Nothing is wrong for everyone, but something can be totally wrong for you.

LESSON: It's imperative that you understand what best meets your overall goals: building a lifestyle business or one that's focused primarily on growth.

Don't Grow Just to Grow

Designing to dress celebrities for the Oscars, Grammys, and New York Fashion Week, heads of state for inaugurations, and regular people for weddings and prom, Stacey Burns-Fox has been operating out of Des Moines, Iowa, since 1993.

Her business, Stacey's Bridal, Prom, and Mastectomy Center, actually started out as a mastectomy center to meet the unique emotional and physical needs of those women. As she grew she added many products and services and says, "I just kept on growing until finally I was like 'oh, ok, now I have an 18,000 square foot building and I have 30-whatever employees and shhhh, I can't do this'!"

She advises new business owners to always have the word "pivot" in their vocabulary. Stacey says, "I didn't learn it early enough. I was always moving forward, moving forward, what did I have to do to move forward, what did I have to do to have the biggest business, what did I have to do to have the best business. I always thought it was taking the next step, I always thought it was expanding, I always thought it was adding to my lines, adding to my store, adding to my offerings. I never realized that sometimes you just have to pivot away from something even though it seems like it's a great idea. Ask yourself what is it really going to add to my bottom line and what is it worth to me to add that to my bottom line? How many more employees will I need and how much personal time is it gonna take?"

Stacey never did that kind of investigation and says, "If I go back and look at historical data, technically I was making a lot more money a couple of moves ago than I am now. Even though it looks big and beautiful, I was actually bringing in more cash with less stress before I made some of the moves."

Now she's realized over the years that her passion is being in the mastectomy room and working one-on-one with those customers, "making sure I can help them with that journey because it's hard and difficult. You're bombarded with so much information you don't even know what to feel, say or do, and you're expected to know everything as a survivor and most don't."

LESSON: Understand what you really want out of the business, where your passions lie, and what you'll need to give up to grow. Then, analyze whether your next step is truly worth it to you in terms of time, money, and stress.

Understand what motivates you

Everyone is motivated by different things like wealth, power, safety, security, recognition, honor, celebrity, and helping others. You'll have a hard time finding your way and motivating yourself until you understand what motivates you.

Sure, we're all motivated by money to a certain extent because we need it to have a house over our head, food on our table, and clothes to wear. Beyond that, though, how much is enough?

Personally speaking, money is a bad motivator for me but making an impact is a good one. Yes, I like money and the things I can do with it, but I've never valued money itself that much. I've always viewed it as replaceable and just numbers. Even when I was a bank auditor sitting in a vault full of cash, it never seemed real.

Here's an illustration of how I differ from many people. Yes, I went into debt to care for my mother at the end of her life but it was worth it to me. The memories I created with her and the nurturing I was able to give back to her, like she gave to my sisters and me growing up, is irreplaceable. There's no amount of money in the world that can buy those memories or that feeling of love.

One day I'll finish paying off the debt but until then it's just a number. I don't obsess over how much the balance is or exactly when I'll be able to pay it off. And, importantly, I don't owe for the things most people do, like cars, boats, and extravagant trips.

It's not that I don't care at all, but it's not important enough for me to ruin my daily life over. I know myself well enough to know that I could easily become totally obsessed with what I owe, that I could become miserable in all other areas of my life just because of that balance due. It's just not worth it.

The "trappings of success" are called that for a reason: it's referring to things that give you an outward appearance of success. You know, the fancy cars and the McMansions, and the debt that goes along with those trappings.

I'd much rather have the trappings of caring for my mother.

> **LESSON:** Understand what's important to you and live your life using that as a guidepost.

Concentrate on ROE and ROS

Years ago Steve Sims measured business success by the traditional ROI, Return on Investment. He was making great money, working with billionaires, traveling the world, but it was extremely stressful and kept him from his family. Now that he understands what it's like to be genuinely fulfilled, he measures it by ROE and ROS: Return on Energy and Return on Smiles.

ROE – Return on Energy: As Steve explains, "When you're speaking to ten people you don't like, your body gets zapped. When working with people you like, it vitalizes you, doesn't tire you, there's no energy draw. This morning I did a 2-hour Zoom call and was exhausted but within seconds of being on with you, I'm energized. You fill up my gas tanks." Now he may have just been saying that to make me feel good, but the comment helped fill up my own gas tanks :)

ROS – Return on Smiles: When Steve sees "people like you suddenly doing more than what you thought you were capable of, seeing the relationships you've been conjuring up, seeing clients doing stuff which they've given themselves permission to do, it makes me smile."

Measuring success and potential clients and projects by using ROE and ROS makes everything an easier decision. You don't need to worry about complicated computations any more. In using these new methods of measurement, Steve says he just innately knows, "this is where I want to be. I want to play on this field."

> **LESSON:** Focusing more inward can help you make better choices and feel more fulfilled in the long run.

Living your best life

Just as your business doesn't have to be built like everyone else's, neither does your life. We're each unique and the way we live our lives should reflect that.

Stacy Huston is a great example of someone who's built a career in an extraordinary way. She says, "If you look at me on paper it seems like I'm doing a lot of different things, and I am. It may not be traditional but it works for me and allows me to thrive and live my best life."

Something her Mom always stressed to her has led Stacy in everything she does: "It doesn't matter if you're cleaning toilets or performing surgery, you should do each of them with incredible integrity and not cut corners, and it will be noticed. And more importantly you'll feel pride in what you do."

Stacy believes you don't have to pick one thing as long as you're able to balance them and give each the time and attention they need when they need it. Most people aren't able to balance their lives like that but she's a master at it. She's actually constructed a very unusual career by fitting together her strengths and using them in different ways for different organizations:

Her main day-to-day job is as Executive Director of Kevin Bacon's Six Degrees organization. Six Degrees does amazing work to amplify the wonderful things that grassroots local charities are doing, giving them the type of exposure they could never get otherwise.

Rather than fundraising for these local charities, Six Degrees helps match them up with celebrities who believe in their cause. Those celebrities can do anything from promote them on social media to what they call a drop-in, where a celebrity who happens to be in the locality will drop in and make a surprise appearance, doing anything from signing autographs to performing live like the Bacon Brothers band has been known to do. The beauty of Six Degrees is that it provides a way that celebrities can more easily help causes in a way that means more than money and is also more fulfilling to them personally.

Because of her experience in a past job, Stacy also consults in the electrical vehicle infrastructure space, building out networks of chargers throughout the country. Her work provides the foundation for electric car owners to be able to access the charging stations they need, which in turn helps boost electric car sales. She's passionate about the environment and working in this industry helps her actively make a difference.

As if all of that isn't enough, Stacy is also the co-founder of Tennyson, where she provides expert advice in working with speakers, curating their messages, pulling out interesting topics, helping them refine what they have to say, and actually producing the talks. While Tennyson is a nonprofit, she doesn't do fundraising for it because that's what she does for Six Degrees.

Although she's very busy, she doesn't try to do everything and be everything to everybody. She has very specific niche focuses within each of her roles, which allows her to manage her time and others' expectations of her. She makes sure she can execute really well at one thing before adding anything else.

And, oh yeah, Stacy is also Mom to her own little girl now, her most important role ever!

LESSON: By concentrating your strengths where they're needed and being vigilant about protecting your time, you can successfully manage multiple roles.

A nudge can be more powerful than a big change

Have you ever noticed how just barely tapping a floating balloon can send it in a drastically different direction? Or how a tiny shift in your car's steering wheel makes a big difference in direction? The same goes for your business.

We often want to make changes but are totally overwhelmed at the thought of where to even start. End result? Paralysis.

Dr. Hoby Wedler is a PhD chemist and entrepreneur who's been on the Forbes Top 30 Under 30 and named a Champion of Change by President Obama. He also happens to have been born blind.

Dr. Hoby knows how much just a slight change in direction in his own movements can drastically alter whether he gets to where he wants to go or not. He applies this philosophy to making changes in his own business, as well as recommendations to clients.

While speaking at a recent Disrupt Your Now conference that Annette Whittenberger (you'll meet her in a bit) and I produced, he remarked "I love the title *Disrupt Your Now* because it's so common that we can find ourselves, and I think a lot of us don't allow ourselves to realize just how common it is, to find ourselves in the position where we're doing a lot of work and we feel really good about what we're doing but maybe it's not exactly what we want to be doing and maybe we need a little nudge, and to nudge us in a slightly different course of action."

"I think it's really motivational," he continues. "I think this whole concept of disruption and taking what we're doing right now, and living in the now, and then just giving it the slightest bump, the slightest disruption - that's powerful and that's motivating. You know, that really lifts us to new places but it's just a little shift in thinking."

Hoby's voice as he says this is so dramatic and motivating. You can hear him for yourself at lisakippsbrown.com/hoby.

I think it's also exciting to not always be doing the same thing; it's fun to adapt and tweak, and change as the world around you changes – or as your own dreams or needs change. You don't have to drop your business and go do something totally different.

I just love the word "nudge" that Hoby uses! Everyone is talking about "pivot" but that often implies bigger changes that seem scary. Everybody can relate to a little nudge.

Dr. Hoby says that when I first told him about *Disrupt Your Now*, he imagined "this, call it a spacecraft or an asteroid, moving through space where there's no gravity and no atmosphere to adjust a path. If you don't touch that little thing that's moving through space it's gonna keep going in the straight line that it's traveling forever and ever. I imagine disrupting one's now as just poking, slightly nudging a spacecraft, so that it still is moving forward in this awesome, amazing way, but just on a slightly different path forward. You can end up with hugely different results."

Aside: In a totally geeky "Squirrel!" moment, I'm laughing inside at how appropriate this analogy is since my nickname for Hoby is Hoby-Wan Kenobi...

> **LESSON:** Don't worry about making huge changes all at once. Making a slight nudge is much less scary, lets you test the waters, and can produce surprising results.

What's your definition of success? BUILD THAT.

This is the crux of the entire book – building your business to meet your own personal definition of success

– but I want to hammer it home.

I asked Brian Bogert, a human behavior and performance coach and founder of Brian Bogert Companies, what his biggest surprise as an entrepreneur has been. He replied "the recipe I always believed delivered success is not really what it was. In my early career, I realized that successful people don't always have the answer, that everyone really does put their pants on the same way."

Brian said he knows "crazy successful people who don't shine in ideas or smarts, and brilliant people who never get into their own stride." I imagine we can all relate to that.

He says the entrepreneurs he knows who get to the levels of success they desire "are the ones that honor, and constantly refine and honor, who they are." They may not shine in the ways we expect, but "they knew who they were, how they were going to show up in the world, what their skillsets were, and what they needed to backfill and leverage. People who don't have clarity can't create, leverage and scale because they don't know their unique gifts."

Reiterating what I've said earlier, he says, "start with you as the person – what are your own goals? Not everyone wants to build a large business."

If you don't know what you want, you can't build it.

And if you build what somebody else wants you're not honoring yourself. You're setting yourself up for misery.

Even if you take nothing else away from this book, please do take away the new habit of viewing everything through the lens of what you want your own life to look like.

> **LESSON:** We can't say it too many times: build a business that helps you reach your own personal goals and your own definition of success. Otherwise, you may as well get a job. At least you can just walk away from that if you get sick of it.

Chapter 4

Most of us have a bad habit of not appreciating just how unique we are so I'm going to remind you:

You are a one-of-a-kind asset to clients, totally unique in the life experiences that combine to make you YOU. Those years of experience comprise great value and make you irreplaceable. Nobody else can offer that set of experiences in that precise combination to the world. Only you. You're more rare than the most sought-after gems.

Now it's time to figure out where you can demand the highest all-around return on your investment in life, but not just in money. Don't forget to include Steve Sims' Return on Energy and Return on Smiles in the equation.

If you're hung up on feeling too old, get over yourself. Exactly which years would you be willing to give up to be younger? You wouldn't have all that valuable experience without living all of those years.

I bet you can remember being a kid and thinking how

cool the older kids were. You couldn't wait to be their age! It's all a matter of perspective and you are now sooo cool.

Or, if you're hung up on feeling too young, remember that youth brings fresh eyes and ideas. The experience of older entrepreneurs combined with your own new thinking can create a powerful combination. It's not the age. It's the attitude. So stop playing by someone else's rules and have the last laugh!

Last year I met a man in his late 50's who had been laid off from work because of the pandemic. He had thought he would be with the company until he retired, but all of a sudden had to look for a job and was obsessed about competing against people much younger. He asked me, "Why would they want to hire me when they can get somebody else for so much less?"

I told him if the company only needs what the less experienced people bring to the table they won't want to hire him. But that means he shouldn't want to work for that company, either. Once I showed him how to market himself like an entrepreneur would market their services, he got it. He stopped playing by the rules of the job search, started playing as an entrepreneur, and got a much better job than his previous one.

LESSON: There are companies who need what only you can bring and people whose lives can be changed by learning from you. Stop discounting your value.

"I've been preparing for this my whole life"

Five years ago Stacy Huston was working full time for a company in the e-car industry when a friend reached out saying the Executive Director of a celebrity nonprofit was going through a life transition and was looking for a replacement. She thought Stacy would be a great fit.

She had always had a lot of empathy. "Growing up as a kid, my mom was the same way. We're very emotional people. We see something, we watch a movie and we cry like that's a family member. I always desired to help and do more but didn't really have the tools or the know-how of how I could make a difference."

But Stacy had moved to Virginia with her current job and was happy with it. Plus, she says, "The LA girl doesn't move all the way to Virginia and end up working for a celebrity. It just didn't seem right!" She also had never worked in a nonprofit, and didn't know if her sales, marketing, and business development experience would be what they needed.

Her friend was persistent, though, and she agreed to have coffee with the then-Executive Director. The very morning of the coffee, her boss in the e-car industry advised her that the company had new investors and was making changes: she had the opportunity to move back to LA, grow with the company, and lead a team, or take a severance package. She had to decide by 3pm that day!

Having recently met the man who is now her husband, she felt that relationship had potential. All of a sudden "that coffee got really important!" The meeting went well and she decided to take the severance.

The organization she was being considered to lead was Kevin Bacon's Six Degrees.

It took about 4 weeks for her to finalize the position but during that time she had a Skype interview with Kevin. "When Skype popped up saying 'Kevin Bacon calling' I was like 'oh, my gosh, this is so weird!' But it was immediately kind of normal. He was really easy to talk to and had passion for what he was doing, but definitely needed some direction with what was next for them."

Although she had doubted her qualifications, she says "I kind of realized through all of my preparation that I did have every skill that they needed. I didn't ever need to run a nonprofit to run a successful one."

She had relationships, business experience, and sales experience. "When you're running a nonprofit you're selling that nonprofit, you're selling programs and initiatives. You're trying to get people to open their wallets to support this vision that you want them to share. When you really start thinking about it, it wasn't that much of a leap."

Stacy says she realized, "I've been preparing for this my whole life." She ended up starting on her birthday :)

> **LESSON:** Skills and talents are portable across industries; the possibilities are limitless.

Are you a voice or an echo?

If you really want to stand out and be noticed, you have to be different. If you're saying what everyone else is saying, why should anyone want to listen to you?

Deeply immersing yourself in something you have a passion for and sharing that enthusiasm with others is one of the best ways to stand out. It can be the beginning of great things for yourself and for others.

Adam White is a perfect example of an entire career being built around his teenage music obsession.

Growing up in the UK in the 60's, Adam was obsessed with America's Motown music. While everyone else was obsessed with the Beatles, he thought, "Why do I want to listen to them? I can see them play anywhere!"

Reading the pop magazines of the day, he saw American charts with the names of Billboard and Cash Box on them and wanted to know more. An Aunt in America sent him some copies and it transformed Adam's world.

Speaking with Adam about this time is mesmerizing to me. I can almost see this British teenager opening the magazines as he transports himself back in time and recounts vivid memories (you can also listen to him speaking of this at lisakippsbrown.com/adam-white):

"You opened those pages and you went to a different world, and that's particularly true about trade magazines because it's business, and so you're drawn into this sort of world about which you know nothing. You don't know who the people are; they're not household names but they essentially run and build stars. You want to know how it's done, particularly if you have a passion for a kind of music, and mine was Motown from an early age."

"I wanted to know everything possible about it from an early age. Who was Berry Gordy? Where is Detroit? Who are Holland-Dozier-Holland? How do you make music like that? Who does it? Where are the musicians? And a trade paper gives you insights you're not going to get anywhere else, particularly not from a distance. Having that opportunity to, if you like, have a business perspective early on when your enthusiasm is driven by music was, I think, both unusual and fortunate."

Adam's first job was as an 18 year-old working in a record store. Most would think they're just selling records to people who want music but Adam, having an awareness of the business side from reading the trade press, convinced the owner that they should start a mail order business. He knew there were "Motown geeks" like him who were deeply in love with the music and the stars, but who couldn't easily feed their hunger for listening to and learning more about either.

To feed this small niche of fans, they began to import Motown records and guaranteed they would stock every Motown record ever released. Customers could buy in the store or through mail order.

Adam even started a weekly newsletter, something very uncommon at the time, updating subscribers on which releases were coming and new imports they had in the store. That let him "legitimately subscribe to Billboard and Cash Box to have information for the newsletter to educate, enthuse and inform even more people around the UK."

All Adam wanted to do was learn more about the music he loved and share it with as many fans as possible. What he didn't realize is that he was already thinking as an entrepreneur.

He was helping to spread the word in the U.K. about Motown, literally building their fan base across the pond in an area where the company's marketing reach was modest, if not invisible.

This was the beginning of Adam becoming known as the authority on Motown. He became a staple in the music industry, working his way up to Editor-in-Chief of Billboard magazine, retiring as Universal Music Group

International's VP of Communications, and writing the book *Motown: The Sound of Young America* with Motown founder Berry Gordy's right-hand man, Barney Ales.

Adam says, "It's been quite a career, fortunate and improbable, but I couldn't have wished for a better one. And most of it has all been in music, largely driven by a piece of music I heard when I was young and took me in a particular direction." That song was Heat Wave by Martha and the Vandellas.

> **LESSON:** Sometimes the things you do get noticed; be ready to leverage that.

Being a night person isn't morally inferior

I've spent so many years beating myself up because I'm a night person. No matter what I do, I'm foggy until mid-day and then I start coming alive. I do my best work late at night when "normal" people are sleeping. My brain is firing on all cylinders then.

And don't bother telling me that it's just a habit. If that were true, I would naturally wake up at 7am every day because my mother spent the first 18 years of my life waking me up at that time.

After years of making myself feel bad for being the way I am I realized, what difference does it make what hours in the day I work? Everybody has the same 24 hours and just because my schedule isn't the same as most people's doesn't mean mine is wrong. As a matter of fact, some early risers I know take naps later in the day. Unless I'm sick, I never take a nap once I'm up so I'm actually USING more hours than some of the early morning snobs.

And what about all the 24-hour businesses out there that have second and third shift workers? The ⅔ who work those shifts aren't lesser people than the first shift workers, and the companies wouldn't be able to operate without them.

Being a night person doesn't make me morally inferior, nor do any of your own personality or biological quirks. Assuming you're not a sociopath.

Stop trying to live like everyone else is – remember, that's what got you to this spot in the first place!

> **LESSON:** It's time to honor yourself and the way you're made.

Your shortcomings are your strengths

As I mentioned in the last chapter, Dr. Hoby Wedler was born blind. His parents didn't raise him any differently than his sighted brother, though. They were both taught that they would get the credit when things go great but they had to take responsibility when things don't work; their failures were their responsibilities and their successes were their own.

If you've never been around someone who is blind you may not realize how refined their other senses become. Sighted people filter out about 85% of what's within their vision and they only scrape the surface of the strengths of their other senses.

Hoby's always loved to cook and experiment with flavors and his sense of taste is highly refined. As a child, his parents would hire him to make large pots of soup that they froze to take to work for lunch. Isn't it wonderful that they encouraged his natural gifts by rewarding him for experimenting?

As an adult those gifts have become apparent through his own work. He believes there's so much value that comes when we temporarily take away eyesight, and encourages the development of sensory literacy: paying attention to all senses to experience the world in a brighter way.

Growing up in the wine country of Sonoma County, California, he developed a passion for wine flavors, accurate descriptions of flavor, and understanding how wine flavor and aroma relate to chemistry. While in graduate school, he was approached by Francis Ford Coppola Winery to create a unique tasting experience for them.

Dr. Hoby created Tasting in the Dark, an event where

blindfolded guests tasted wines and tried to describe the flavors and aromas, and guess what each wine was. It became so popular, Francis Ford Coppola Winery rolled it out into an education program for its sales team and Hoby has also expanded it into other industries.

Just before the pandemic shutdown he collaborated on a Tasting in the Dark with the Culinary Institute of America and Dave Matthews' label Dreaming Tree Wines. In a double-blind tasting, four Dreaming Tree wines were paired with five different Dave Matthews' songs to demonstrate how music affects the sense of taste.

In a trick pairing, the last wine was a rosé that was secretly paired back-to-back with two different songs. On the second pour, only 2 of 120 participants correctly guessed that the wine was a rosé. Most everyone else thought it was a white wine and probably Chardonnay.

Wedler said, "The music transformed the wine into something completely different. The crowd was blown away, because they would never have guessed that this was the same wine."

Now Dr. Hoby is busy preparing to launch his own brand of gourmet seasoning blends which will be the first seasonings with Braille labels.

Hoby says, "Entrepreneurship is a lot like being a blind person in a sighted world. We entrepreneurs have to constantly find new ways to do things and how to solve problems."

LESSON: Identify what's perceived as your greatest shortcomings to help uncover your greatest strengths.

"It's like making lawn art"

Des Moines-based Trevor Johnson has owned his lawncare business for 3 years now and has gone from a one-man shop with one customer to having an assistant. With no active marketing whatsoever, he's taken business in high-end neighborhoods from large, established companies. He's making money hand over fist and still has more people wanting to switch to him. He doesn't even have time to spend all the money he's making.

How did he get all this business? When a customer's neighbor saw what a great job he did, he told Trevor he does a much better job than the company he'd been using. He wanted his yard to look as neat as his neighbor's, with the precise cutting lines and neat edges that Trevor delivers, and hired Trevor on the spot.

After that, other neighbors took notice and realized their lawns were looking pretty shabby compared to the two Trevor was caring for. Gradually his business spread from street to street without him even trying to pick up new customers. His work spoke for itself and everyone wanted what he was delivering.

You're probably wondering "what's the big deal? It's lawncare." Well, Trevor is only 17 years old and is on the autism spectrum. His mind is a cross between an engineer and artist, so he's great at mechanical work like building complex Lego projects with moving parts but also appreciates beauty.

He started his business when he was just 14, when that neighbor saw what a great job he did for his first customer – his parents. He's also my cousin, but that's not why I'm including him here. I'm including him to show you that being true to the way your mind operates and not trying to force yourself into a box will let your talents and strengths shine through, and can bring you more business than you would dare dream of.

His customers don't hire him because they feel sorry for him. They hire him because his work is head and shoulders above the big companies since he's so into symmetry, lines, and neatness. He's meticulous, while hourly employees of competitors deliver half-ass quality so they can quickly get to the next job.

When he was on my live show, my co-host asked what his favorite part of the business is. His answer was that "it's like making lawn art." To him, his work is meant to make something beautiful, not to just cut the grass. There's a huge difference in results when you're doing something just to be doing it, and doing it to create art.

Trevor's assistant is currently his father, who's an executive in a financial company. He'll be 18 soon and is deciding whether to go to college in another state. The great thing is, even if he's in another state, he could restart this business there and have customers lining up once again just because of the quality of his work.

> **LESSON:** Honoring your strengths and the things you enjoy provides the foundation for you to stand out from the competition.

"I'm so thankful I was born blind"

If you're a sports fan you may have heard of Aaron Golub: he became the first legally blind person to play NCAA Division I football when he was a three-year letterman long snapper at Tulane University. After college he became an NFL free agent before deciding to become a financial investment advisor.

You'll learn more about Aaron later in Chapter 12, but you may be surprised at his view of being blind. He says, "I'm so thankful, I'm so blessed, I'm so happy that I was born legally blind because I've met so many incredible people because of it, met so many amazing people because of it. If I wasn't legally blind maybe I wouldn't have the drive, the ambition, the attitude I have today. I think I'm going to see a lot more success in my life simply because I was born legally blind."

Aaron has advice to help you overcome obstacles: "Too many people think things in life happen 'to' them and they're a victim; they already set themselves behind. If you think of things happening 'for' you, you're putting yourself ahead because you understand it happens for a reason – it's a challenge, to help you grow and learn."

The next time you're having a pity party over something, put it in perspective by reminding yourself of Aaron's words.

LESSON: We can turn challenges in our lives into assets that make us stronger.

LISA KIPPS-BROWN

PART TWO - Expanding Your Network & Mind

Chapter 5

It's amazing that using the same skills and experience with just a different set of clients who have different goals can transform your life.

In Chapter 1 you learned how the outside challenge of writing a book helped Steve Sims realize that his talents and experience were portable. Now you'll see why that made such a difference in his and his family's life.

In his first business, he says he loved the challenge of spending a billionaire's money to give them a cool cocktail story and "I would love every single point of it up until the brag." That's when the thrill was gone for him. Then the book helped him realize he "could change people's lives instead of just creating a brag factor." He had never even realized that was an option for him.

He says, "I've been in rooms all over the world –

Monaco, Macau – where I would hear a billionaire boast about what he did to another billionaire, only to get some kind of pecking order as to who's cooler. I'm sitting at the bar thinking, *I did that, but I no longer like what I did because I'm seeing it being used for bad*."

When he was able to begin working with entrepreneurs, though, suddenly his work became so much more fun and personally fulfilling. "Working with an entrepreneur and using that same energy, that person isn't bragging, that person is doing. And when it improves their relationship with their family and the people they employ, it improves those people's relationships and the company is more productive, and they're smiling. It's so much more rewarding."

Using his skills in a way that was more personally fulfilling also naturally improved Steve's family life. "It made a big change to my relationship with my wife and my family because, you're right, there were a lot of times we would make a lot of money working with a very powerful person but I was grumpy. I had all the new toys, I had the beautiful house but I had this grumpy demeanor. There were times I'd be in a penthouse suite in Rome, being flown around by private jet and it was all being paid for by the client, and I would do it with a grumpy scowl because, without realizing it, I was depressed. This was not a good place to be and I'm very happy that I broke out of it."

Growing up in England, Steve used to watch a TV show called "Only Fools and Horses" in which "the main character sold stuff out of his car and called himself an entrepreneur. That's how entrepreneurs used to be looked at. If you were an entrepreneur it's because you couldn't get a real job; you were substandard. Now they're the new rockstars and idols."

We're lucky to live in a unique time in our history, when pretty much anyone can start a business and work with clients throughout the world doing something they love. We don't have to invest in large inventories or maintain a large office and bloated staff. It's up to you to find your own happy place, though.

LESSON: Take the time now to figure out the sandbox you're really meant to be in, where you can work with people you sincerely enjoy, use your skills to make the most impact, and experience business in a way that will be the most personally fulfilling to you.

Don't let your education limit you

College is expensive so it's natural for you to feel like you have to stay in the field you studied even if you're miserable. Remember that you took classes in many subjects, though! A decision made in your youth shouldn't prevent you from at least exploring other possibilities... You never know what you might find.

Bernard Evans studied Electrical Engineering and had a

lucrative career working for companies like Texas Instruments on Top Secret projects for the government. The problem was, he was tired of knowing that his income potential would always be capped when working for someone else, they would own any intellectual property he created, and he was bored.

One weekend a couple of friends came to visit him in Dallas from New York City. Knowing he had paid his way through college by working as a barber, they invited him to meet a new musical artist who was coming to St. Louis to perform and was looking for an image consultant. He thought *what do I know about image consulting*? But his friends were insistent that he at least go meet her and give her feedback.

The performer was Whitney Houston, whose career was just beginning to explode. Meeting her set off a chain of events that resulted in him leaving the field of engineering, becoming a licensed cosmetologist, owning his own exclusive salon, creating his own line of products for multicultural hair textures, and working with a long list of celebrities. His clients included Luther Vandross, Mary J. Blige, Sade, LaToya Jackson, Joan Rivers, Madonna, Teddy Pendergrass, Phylicia Rashad, Stephanie Mills and many more.

He's been featured in magazines like Vogue, Essence, and Jet, and his salons include Color Explosion Hair Salon in New York City, Platinum Artistes by Bernard

Evans in London, and BeYofi Hair Bar & Salon in Atlanta. In a quest to help other entrepreneurs, he's also created his K.A.S.H. (Knowledge, Attitude, Skills, Habits) system, wrote a book on the topic, and is in the process of developing new training materials for clients.

Bernard realized that being educated and skilled as an engineer didn't mean he had to stay stuck forever in a field that was unfulfilling to him. It's funny that we're both the same age, both in the first generation of our families to go to college, and both ended up ditching our degrees for something that made us happier. While we're thankful for our education, we recognize that it doesn't define us. Life is about more than a degree.

> **LESSON:** Don't let career decisions you made at a very young age lock you in and prevent you from even exploring other possibilities. Part of education is about keeping an open mind.

Shatter your own glass ceiling

We always hear about employees having a glass ceiling but we don't realize that we often create our own glass ceilings, even if we're the business owner. I've already shared how Steve Sims took his skillset to a new arena and increased his happiness, but now you can learn how he had already freed up his earning potential.

In 2005 his company, Bluefish, was making a lot of money. Steve says, "We'd just finished being the official concierge for the Kentucky Derby, the Grammys, and New York Fashion Week. I had 30 staff members and a 5000 square foot office. One day I was going through payroll asking what everyone does, what do they turn over. It seems like everyone is always 'working on something' but it's not coming in."

In reviewing the books, Steve "realized we'd bring a client in and make $5,000 but I'd spent $6,000 on payroll. I'm like 'hang on a minute, you owe me a thousand dollars!' I realized I was hiring all these staff to appear to be successful when, funnily enough, I already was. So, I did a mass sacking and we got down to like 12 people in one week. I realized the really successful business is one that's lean enough to be as impactful as possible and able to pivot as it needs."

He cut down to no office, 5 staff members, a skeleton crew, and had no liabilities. "Then we hit the recession and it was such a glorious time for me. You may think having an office with 100 people working for you is good, but the real smart person is the one who has 2 people on payroll: no liability, no worry, no stress. Like me and you, they have a laptop opened up on the kitchen table but can still do a 200 grand deal without it costing them 300 grand."

By getting rid of all the fluff and the staff that weren't contributing to his bottom line, Steve was able to shatter his own glass ceiling.

> **LESSON:** High revenues are meaningless if it's all flowing back out the door for overhead. Check your ego, clean house, and shatter your own glass ceiling.

What's your canary in the coal mine?

Richard Mulholland is one of those people whose brain always has to be in "solve mode." In 2019 he played board games all the time to provide the challenge his brain needed. When COVID hit in 2020 and the shutdown began, all of a sudden he had a real challenge: how to keep his business afloat.

After a while he realized he was rarely playing those board games he loved. Why? You probably think it was just because he didn't have time, but Richard says it's because he didn't need the mental challenge any more to allow his brain to be in solve mode. He had it every day in adapting his business and, as a result, was growing at a faster rate than he ever had during the decades since he'd started the business.

He hadn't realized how bored he'd become since his company was so successful and on cruise control pre-COVID. Now he says, "This will be my canary in the coal mine: if I find myself playing games 5 to 6 times a week I'll know I'm not doing anything meaningful in my business."

We work so hard to become successful that we lose sight

of the challenges we loved along the way. In Richard's words, "At some point you stopped being an entrepreneur and you started running a business. Running a business is crap."

Being an entrepreneur is all about fixing a problem or filling a gap and Richard's mistake had been that, because he had grown bored in the company, he "kept starting other companies instead of trying to make my actual company better. Now I want my business to be dangerous – not harmless." In other words, he wants to continually be in solve mode, pushing the envelope to challenge his own industry to reach new heights.

> **LESSON:** Knowing your own canary in the coal mine gives you the ability to head off problems early and make changes that may be needed for you to be more fulfilled in the business.

There's gotta be a pony in this pile of doodoo

Before you ditch your business model or clients, it's always a good practice to check your own attitude. That can be one of the easiest things to change if it's holding you back from enjoying the business more.

Serial tech entrepreneur Daryl Hatton is the founder of ConnectionPoint, one of the first crowdfunding-as-a-service companies, with the brands FundRazr, Sponsifi, and CoCoPay. He strongly believes that focusing on the results you're creating for customers you like, rather than focusing on yourself, will make a huge difference in the quality of your experience in the business.

Daryl finds "it'll change the way customers look at you. If they think you're actually enjoying helping them and they're loving that, then bonds form that supercede lowest price, supercede speed to market. They really are a lot stronger. We are still humans and we still buy from people most of the time."

He tells the story of two young guys shoveling manure. One is complaining while the other is whistling a tune. The complainer looks at the whistler and says, "What's with you? We're in here shoveling crap." The whistler replies, "Well, with all this manure there has to be a pony around here we can ride!"

Daryl knows that "it's really hard to have a purpose to get up for if you hate what you're doing or who you're doing it for. It can be scary to go, 'we should do something different,' but the whole point here is maybe you can take just a small change, take a look at what you're doing in a different way, maybe reframe your perspective on it, and it might change the outcome a lot."

He says one of the things that has helped him to live more positively and in the now was to practice gratitude. "When I was able to remember something in the moment, particularly, that I was grateful for, I've got a lot more things to be grateful for all of a sudden. At the end of the day, that was a good day! That moment of gratitude helped make the day a success." And that sets up the next day to be more likely to be successful.

> **LESSON:** You can never go wrong by checking to see if your own attitude is part of the problem.

It's okay to say no

Reminding you to check your own attitude doesn't mean that the customer is always right. The fact is, you should be very picky about who you allow to even be your customer. Everyone isn't right for you and you're not right for everyone; just like in dating, you have the right to say thanks but no thanks.

If someone is already your customer that doesn't mean you have to be stuck with them if you realize it's not a good match. Keeping the wrong customers can make life miserable for you and your team, and can destroy your own company culture.

Kerry Edelstein is founder of Research Narrative, a full service market research and consumer insights agency specializing in the communications, media, digital technology, and entertainment sectors. She says they had a client for years who truly valued their partnership, but over time "the client became a disrespectful bully to me and to our employees – it began to feel like an abusive relationship. I sensed that this individual had been on the receiving end of shouting and derogatory language at past jobs, and had unwittingly normalized that behavior. We broached our operating and conversational norms many times, but over time it became clear that this client wasn't capable of changing their behavior. And I couldn't let that toxicity continue to permeate and jeopardize the collaborative business culture I'd worked so hard to achieve. I was like 'this isn't worth it to me; you're literally screaming at our team over PowerPoint slides. I mean, a little perspective is in order.' So eventually I just doubled the price of the contract knowing they'd say no. And they did indeed decline to re-up, and we all moved on without any ill will."

She and her team also had conversations about the temperaments they're willing to endure, which helped them better screen for that. No outsider should be able to destroy morale in your own company.

It's not just about temperament, though. You also need the right kind of clients from a decision-making capacity. Kerry says, "sometimes we'll get hired in by people who are either so senior that they don't pay attention, so it's really hard to get their attention to do our jobs, or so junior that we can give them all the brilliant insights in the world but they don't have the internal authority to activate those insights. Our sweet spot is somebody senior enough that they have that power and authority, but not so senior that we can't get them on the phone."

If you're having issues with your own clients, you need to take a step back and look at who you're working with, what you're doing for them, and how all of that aligns with your own vision and goals. Remember, not every client deserves to work with you. There are plenty of companies that are a better fit for them, and plenty of clients who are a better fit for you. Keeping an abundance mindset will help you recognize the right clients and the ones to run from.

LESSON: Choose your clients wisely and remember you always have the right to say no.

Chapter 6

A common thread throughout conversations I've had with dozens and dozens of successful entrepreneurs is to always be ready for opportunity.

You never know when it will come knocking, and if you're not ready when it does the loss is yours.

It may take many years of hard work before it seems to magically raise its head, leaving people who don't know you to think you're an overnight success. On the other hand, it could literally come out of nowhere, like a stroke of luck and you just happened to be in the right place at the right time.

Personally, though, I don't believe in coincidences and I think you make your own luck. The story of how my cousin Charles Kipps broke into the entertainment industry is a perfect example.

When he was just in high school, Charles wrote for a local weekly newspaper, the Salem (VA) Times Register. There wasn't much exciting going on locally, but he convinced the paper's owner into letting him interview popular artists who were performing at the Roanoke Civic Center, artists like Herman's Hermits, Mitch Ryder & The Detroit Wheels, Sam & Dave, and Otis Redding. After interviewing the performers, he always made sure to get business cards from their managers and agents. He said, "I had this stack of business cards but I didn't know what I was going to do with them."

One day while in his early twenties he was walking down the street in Washington, DC, and heard an interesting song coming through a window. Walking in, he saw three African-American gentlemen around a piano, "and I told them I wanted to take a demo tape to New York and see what I could do with it. They looked at me like, you know, you're just a little skinny kid."

They agreed to let him try, though, and he called one of the people whose business cards he had collected, the manager of Mitch Ryder & The Detroit Wheels. That manager referred him to Ron Moseley at Sussex Records who asked him to bring the recording to New York, so Charles jumped on a plane with his little mono recording like what would have been used to take dictation on. The group was The Presidents and the song was "5-10-15-20 (25-30 Years of Love)," which went on to become a Grammy-nominated Top 10 hit.

Sussex Records hired Van McCoy as the song's

producer and he and Charles ended up writing songs under McCoy/Kipps Productions, working together for almost ten years with artists like Aretha Franklin, Gladys Knight & The Pips, and Melba Moore. McCoy wrote the monster hit "The Hustle," being inspired to write it after Charles saw people doing a dance called the Hustle at the Adam's Apple nightclub. Charles also wrote "Walk Away From Love," David Ruffin's only post-Temptations hit, and is a Grammy-Nominated record producer with seven Gold Records.

None of this would have happened if he hadn't been ready when he heard the Presidents singing through that window. He had talked the newspaper owner into letting him report on the Civic Center, collected and hung on to business cards, recognized an opportunity when he happened to hear the song, and then went after what he wanted. He also turned the Civic Center reporting into an award-winning interview with the legendary New York Yankee Mickey Mantle!

This is just the beginning of Charles' long and varied career in entertainment, which you'll read more about in Chapter 7. He describes himself as "a 6'8" tumbleweed," which I think is hilarious but so apt. He just naturally attracts and collects opportunities wherever he rolls through.

LESSON: You create your own luck by constantly seeking out opportunity and being ready to seize it when you find it.

One business's junk is another business's gold mine

After Shawn Barksdale started the job at the printing company, the ex-con was helping his supervisor with spring cleaning around the business: removing old equipment and supplies that they knew they didn't need.

Noticing a machine sitting in the corner, Shawn asked what it was.

Supervisor: "A T-shirt machine."

Shawn: "How much you want for it?"

Supervisor: "Take it."

Shawn: "Take it where?"

Supervisor: "Take it home."

He had no clue what he had been given, just "a T-shirt machine." Lying in bed with his wife that night he searched YouTube for "T-shirt making machine" and saw an image of a machine exactly like the one he had brought home. After watching the video and seeing the machine being used he looked at his wife and said, "they gave me a gold mine!"

He really didn't know what he would do with it, but about a week later he got up at 4:30am with a pad and pen and wrote a business plan (I'm starting to see a pattern here with Shawn and a pad and pen!). He wrote down things like: What are you going to call the business? Who's going to help you start it? What business type should it be?

He didn't know anything about LLC's or other business types but says he "found that when you try to help yourself, people help you. There are very good people in the world; you just have to connect to those people."

Shawn is now the founder of Press 4 Time Tees, host of his own podcast called "Ten Minutes of Truth," and a powerful motivational speaker. His podcast features guests that he talks with about topics that frequently aren't discussed in the home, like trauma and suicide, in an effort to help others.

Recalling starting his business, he says "I didn't know anything about marketing, either. All I knew was, I knew how to talk. People marveled, not so much at the designs at the time because I didn't really know what I was doing. It was more so that I was the brand. It was me more than the T-shirts."

Of course there were the inevitable naysayers who would make comments like "it's just a matter of time before he goes back in." Shawn says, "That's my fuel even now. It's the level up."

His success has inspired a lot of other people to make T-shirts and he knows they're thinking, "If Shawn's doing it, it must be easy. This dude ain't gonna do nothing too hard." He doesn't care, though. He's just happy that he's inspired them.

We live in the same community and, on a personal note, I want to give a shout out to the local company that helped Shawn get his entrepreneurial start: Benton Thomas Office Supplies, owner Mickey Thomas, and Shawn's then-supervisor Barry Long. I love that they gave him a chance and only cared that he had the qualifications for the job they needed done.

> **LESSON:** Keep your eyes open because you never know when an opportunity might arise, even if you don't recognize it.

Look for signs on the long and winding road

Before Jeffrey Madoff became one of the Top 10 fashion designers in the US or started Madoff Productions through which he collaborates with clients like Ralph Lauren, Victoria's Secret, Tiffany, Radio City, and Harvard University, he was a student at University of Wisconsin. He never realized that a frustrating classroom experience would decades later help lead him to teaching, writing a book, and becoming a playwright and theatre producer.

The Vietnam War was raging and so were conflicts at home. Protests were common throughout the country over the war itself, desegregation, and civil rights. A student with a double major in Philosophy and Psychology, Jeffrey was sitting in his Political Science classroom there in Madison when he looked out the window and saw tanks, State Troopers, and the National Guard responding to a protest.

Frustrated about the obvious disconnect between the real world and the classroom, he vented to the professor: "All this activity outside of our windows that's happening, we're in a Political Science class and the most current book you have us reading is 10 years old! You're not giving us any of the tools to understand what's happening right outside the windows here."

Not taking kindly to the undergraduate's confrontation, the professor challenged him to teach the class if he thought he could do it so much better. Jeffrey replied that he wasn't prepared that day but he'd be ready the next week...

When the professor and students arrived in class the next week, they found he was indeed prepared. He had brought Senators Gaylord Nelson and William Proxmire, and the first black candidate for sheriff of a major city. He brought political science to life in the classroom.

Years later in New York City, he was asked to do a guest lecture at Parsons School of Design. His lecture was so well-received, the professor invited him back every semester for four years and his popularity led to him being offered a position as an Adjunct Professor.

Drawing on his experience in that Wisconsin classroom decades before, Madoff realized he wanted to teach the kind of course he would want to take. The result was Creative Careers, a course that lets students hear from and ask questions of a different highly accomplished artist, entrepreneur, or business leader each week; Oscar, Emmy, Tony and Pulitzer Prize winners, people like Daymond John, Kathy Ireland, Dan Sullivan, Joe Polish, and Randi Zuckerburg.

Until he started this course nobody could imagine why creatives would want business advice but it's one of the most popular courses at Parsons School of Design and has been fully booked since he started it in 2007.

Madoff's bestselling book *Creative Careers: Making a Living With Your Ideas* came out of this course and features advice from his own experiences as well as from over 40 of his guest speakers.

He's also written the play "Personality: The Lloyd Price Musical", based on the life of the Rock and Roll Hall of Fame member, which will have its world premiere in 2022.

Take it from Jeffrey, "The long and winding road gets you to where you're going and sometimes you don't know where you're going."

> **LESSON:** You don't have to have your life's journey
> completely mapped out to be successful and fulfilled.
> It's a unique tapestry that you can create as you go.

The right mindset leads to the right opportunities

Before founding BrEpic Communications and writing
the book Epic Business, Justin Breen was a journalist. In
2018, after starting BrEpic, he'd "made more money in a
year than he ever thought possible" but found he'd
"never been more miserable."

Justin thought, "That doesn't make sense .. all this
money and I don't even have the same happiness as
before. 1+1 doesn't equal 2. 10+10 equals -500; that's
what it really was. I learned that spending time with my
family is what makes me happy."

That doesn't mean he gave up on making money, though.
I asked him what he changed in his business and he said
"Nothing. I worked on my mindset and my brain. That's
what I worked on. The right mindset leads to the right
network which creates the right opportunities. All this
other stuff is meaningless."

Thankfully Justin recognized how he felt very early on
in his entrepreneurial journey and didn't make the long-
term mistakes that too many of us make. He was strong
enough to confront the situation and figure out how he

could be happy again. He has a business he loves and a full family life because he built the business in a way that suits him personally.

He says, "I've known multiple billionaires and gajillionaires and I ask them 'how's your family?' and they say they never see them. I see the look in their eyes or hear it in their voice or see it through a virtual pause... I'm not one of those people. I never will be."

Justin didn't need to be told it's his business and he can make it anything he wants. He knew that owning a business that made him unhappy was not only pointless but destructive, and he took the time to get back on track early.

> **LESSON:** Prioritize what's important to you and build your business around that rather than building your life around your business.

Moments that seem random can transform your life

Remember Adam White in the "Are you a voice or an echo?" story from Chapter 4? He's the British kid who was so obsessed with Motown that he helped its acceptance and popularity in the U.K. He didn't think about it that way, though; he just loved the music and wanted to connect with others like him.

I've got a couple of stories to share of how Adam

created his own opportunities just because of his love of Motown.

A big British pop paper, New Musical Express (NME), had charted a record by a Motown artist. Adam says, "They put some line in the paper that they didn't know who this guy was. Well, I did – surprise, surprise. I knew this guy's name was R. Dean Taylor and I knew enough about him to say 'well look, here's some information you can use.' They paid me for it. They printed an article with my name on it and I got 2 guineas at the time, which was 2 pounds and 2 shillings, the first money I earned as a journalist."

Adam's experience is a perfect example of something Richard Mulholland told me. "If you know something that somebody else doesn't know but needs to know, that has tremendous cache and value and you have to work out a way to allow yourself to give them knowledge. You don't want to *get into* a business, you want to *give into* a business."

He could have just read the article and gone about his day, but Adam took the time to share information with an established music publication that they didn't know and didn't take the time to find out. He delivered value without expecting anything in return, what you hear so much about as "the give mentality" now. It's nothing new.

Another "piece of good fortune" Adam had while working in the record store happened one evening when he went to London to see Gladys Knight & The Pips. Adam shares that "after the show I went down the road to a pub and who should be in the pub but a guy called Barney Ales, the Vice President of Motown records. Because I had been reading Motown and Cash Box all those years, I knew who this dude was. I went up and introduced myself. I mean why wouldn't you, right? I think he was stunned that this young Brit knew who he was."

It's amazing that Adam was able to meet such a pivotal figure in his favorite music at a local pub where nobody else knew who he was. He told me, "I wasn't to know he would come back in my life in subsequent years, but it was one of those opportunities that happens. It's a coincidence but it was a remarkable step along the way."

Yes, truly remarkable because decades later Adam and Barney would partner to write the book *Motown: The Sound of Young America*, the definitive book on the upstart company from Detroit that disrupted the music industry.

Adam shared two lessons that he learned in the music business and I think they apply in most businesses:

- when you're smart in the music business you also have to be lucky, and

- you'll be amazed what you can achieve if you're willing to give others the credit.

Reflecting on his early years and how his love of Motown turned into a very successful career, Adam said, "Those early moments when it seems random, depending on how you deal with it, can change your life and form your life in subsequent years."

> **LESSON:** Look for opportunities to make others smarter and don't be afraid to reach out to important companies or people.

Chapter 7

"The best thing I ever did was go to Elaine's."

Connecting with connectors can work magic, and the six degrees of separation theory says that you're within reach of almost anyone.

I'm only 2 degrees from the Queen of Malaysia, Elon Musk, Ralph Lauren, and Kevin Bacon, which means that you're 3 degrees if you know me. But I digress.

I shared in Chapter 6 how my cousin Charles Kipps turned a high school job writing for the local paper into owning a production company that worked with some of the top music acts of the 70's. Now it's time to share how he turned that into the work he really wanted to do: screenwriting.

In the late 70's the music world was becoming so corporate the thrill was gone for Charles. Being able to meet with one person to make a deal had turned into long meetings with a room full of suits who only cared about whether they thought a song would be commercially successful (foreshadowing the industry's comeuppance). Screenwriting had always been his goal, anyway, so he set about figuring out how he could put himself in the right place to meet people who had those connections.

Charles knew "the literati were all at Elaine's Restaurant" on the Upper East Side so that became the focus of his strategy.

If the name Elaine's rings a bell, the restaurant has been featured in pop culture over the years. The lyrics of Billy Joel's song "Big Shot" included, "they were all impressed with your Halston dress and the people that you knew at Elaine's," it's been in a number of movies and TV shows, and it was the favorite meeting and dining place for Stuart Woods' title character in the Stone Barrington novels.

Charles showed up at Elaine's one evening for cocktails and chatted with a few people. When he came back a couple of nights later, Elaine pointed at him across the room signaling "you – come here." He's hard to miss because he's 6'8" tall, but Elaine was also notorious for getting to know her customers and booting the ones she didn't like.

Luckily for Charles, she took a liking to him and proceeded to introduce him to many connected people, kicking off the next phase of his career writing for TV and the big screen. For over 30 years Elaine's was his go-to spot where, like Stone Barrington, he held meetings and struck deals.

Charles has had two major inflection points in his career, both of which came from putting himself in the position to meet people of influence, first by reporting on concerts at the Roanoke Civic Center and second by going to Elaine's.

He told me, "The best thing I ever did was go to Elaine's." The connections he made there led directly to work that won him awards like the Emmy, Peabody, Humanitas, and Edgar. Among his varied portfolio is writing and producing the only Law & Order television movie ever made, Exiled, which was credited by the creator as giving him the idea for the Law & Order franchise. He's also written a number of novels and nonfiction books, including Cop Without a Badge, which was used as the plot line for an episode of Real Housewives of New Jersey.

LESSON: When you know what you want to achieve and the types of people you need to meet to make the right connections, you can put yourself in a strategic position to meet them.

Surround yourself with the right people

Stacey Burns-Fox always advises entrepreneurs to surround themselves with the right people, people who know what you don't and those who understand what you're trying to do.

She told me, "When I first started my business I had a great lawyer, I had a great insurance guy, I had a great accountant, but I didn't think anything about interviewing my bankers. I didn't realize I could. I thought you just went to the bank that you had your money in and that was it. I didn't realize I had a choice. Well, my banker didn't believe in me and even though I had an SBA guarantee, they refused to fund the SBA loan."

Starting her business with just $183 and convincing "a whole bunch of people to give me a whole bunch of credit," she was in the black within 8 months. On not getting the SBA loan, Stacey admits "I can only look back at that and say that was my fault. I didn't have the banker on my side. I didn't convince the banker of my skills, and my ability to have a good business, and my ability to pay the loan back, so that's my fault."

> **LESSON:** Don't just interview potential employees. Also interview those who will provide the professional support you need to succeed, and make sure they truly understand you and your strengths and goals.

You have to have people who push you

Brandon Straza was feeling unfulfilled. He had built an insurance company with 8,000 clients and 7-figure annual revenues, followed by exiting a successful sale of his ownership in a company doing over 2 billion a year in lending. Now he was ready for the next thing but didn't know what that was. Feeling like he had stopped learning for the past 20 years, he decided to attend a mastermind in Thailand.

People kept asking why he was spending money and time away from his business. They didn't think it made sense for him to go, but he had people who could run the business and he was hungry for change.

He was overwhelmed by the caliber of people he met in Thailand, though, people like Steve Sims whom you read about earlier. Brandon didn't feel like he was an entrepreneur because he thought anyone could build the business he did. He had total imposter syndrome and was bombarded with thoughts like "I don't belong here. I'm a business owner, not an entrepreneur. Look at everything they're doing."

Stuck in the airport at midnight when his return flight was cancelled, Brandon was miserable. He just wanted to be home with his family, but it seems that cancellation was meant to be. In the hours he spent alone, he got over his doubts. He started thinking, "I AM an entrepreneur. I'm here to stay, I'm here to play."

He says, "I actually started wearing that cloth, those shoes, when I was in Thailand but then I thought there's gotta be other people like me. They've stopped learning or want to learn and don't know who to learn from."

His true entrepreneurial spirit came alive and right there in the airport he started registering domain names for an idea he had begun to formulate. He had realized "Marketers are better at marketing than the real coaches and real masterminds. Marketers are the noise. The signal is what we want the consumer to hear. I want to cut out the noise so members can hear the signal, and help match them with the right coach or mastermind."

Brandon says, "I looked at how Steve and others were successful, pulled out pieces from each and basically asked myself 'how could I take a Scrabble word and rearrange it into something that could help other people?' "

That idea is now The Success Finder, a platform that helps entrepreneurs learn through free content provided by expert coaches that Brandon and his team have vetted, including me, Steve, and a few others in this book. If a member wants to hire a coach, the platform has tools to help them find the best fit but they're never required to buy anything.

Brandon is building something that didn't exist, to help others like him who know they want to learn but worry about wasting money on the wrong person. He believes, "Whether someone is investing $500 or $5000 in coaching, it's equally important. They need a rating, matching, knowledge-based center that will bring members, coaches, and masterminds together."

It's also a for-purpose business, reinvesting in members and building a nonprofit arm to help develop young entrepreneurs.

The Mastermind Effect podcast is a byproduct of building The Success Finder. Hosting the podcast allowed him to interview experts to see if they're the right people for the platform. "It allowed me to have conversations with people who would have shut the door if I had just asked them to be part of The Success Finder."

Brandon has found a way to help the entrepreneur who's thinking "how do I know when I make that investment in myself that it's the right person?"

He's truly come into his own and his wife now tells him, "You're no CEO, you're Walt Disney."

LESSON: Just being around people who are more successful than you helps challenge your thought patterns and can truly push you to new heights.

Mentors provide shortcuts

Being able to learn from other people's failures and successes is like getting a master class in entrepreneurship. When you apply what you learn to capitalize on their successes and avoid mistakes of your own, you've got a shortcut to success.

Many entrepreneurs don't realize the importance of this and I have to say I used to be one of them. I was so tied up in raising my kids and running my business, I didn't take time to think of much else. Don't get me wrong, I read tons of entrepreneurial books but there's nothing quite like talking with someone who's already been where you are, has created their own success, made their own mistakes, and can give objective feedback on what you're thinking and doing. The human connection is so important.

Brian Bogert is another one who didn't see it earlier. He says, "I wish I would have started investing in myself sooner. The outside lens helps me move faster and with less effort. I would have shaved off years of heartache and pain if I'd brought in coaches sooner."

A good coach doesn't give you the answers or do it for you. They challenge your perspective and ask the right questions to help move you along on your journey. "I wish I would have realized how many things I didn't know," Brian said. "I didn't know what I didn't know, and if I'd brought in an outside lens sooner it would have shortened my path considerably."

Brian not knowing what he didn't know touches on

something I talk about in the next chapter, that the most important questions are the ones you don't even know need to be asked. This is a fundamental point and I really can't stress it too much.

If you didn't get the message clearly in the preceding story with Brandon Straza talking about why he started The Success Finder, I'll remind you now that not just any coach will do. You need to find one who not only has the type of experience that will benefit you but also has a personality and style of communication that meshes with you. Otherwise you're wasting money and time and can actually end up worse off. (shameless plug for a great platform: join The Success Finder for free and get a headstart on finding your perfect coach!)

> **LESSON:** Investing in yourself by working with the right coaches and masterminds can be the best investment you'll ever make, with an ROI that greatly exceeds anything.

You're never too small to have a procurement expert

All businesses can benefit from saving on expenses to boost the bottom line, but when most people think of procurement they think of three things:

- old-style purchasing departments in large companies who order everything staff needs and dole it out,

- large companies that negotiate massive contracts, or

- slashing costs to the bone when a company is trying to restructure or make itself appear more financially healthy for a potential sale.

It's not the type of service that the average small business thinks they can benefit from. But what if I told you working with the right procurement expert could help you do things like save almost 50% on cost of goods sold without changing vendors? And you're never too small to see those kinds of benefits.

Mark Milen founded Innovate Holdings just before COVID hit to provide strategic spend management for clients ranging from small businesses with $1M annual revenue to Fortune 500 companies.

Through 2020, Innovate's clients' average ROI was 17x investment, meaning for every dollar they spent with Innovate they saved $17!

Here's a couple of examples of how they've helped small businesses:

- a marketing firm needed 5 new Macbooks; the average price was $2400 each but they thought they could get them for $2200 each. They told Innovate they'd hire them to do the deal if they could get them for less than that. Mark's team negotiated lease terms of only $34.60/month per laptop with the first 6 months of payments waived, and the deal includes AppleCare support and new laptops every 3 years at no extra charge!

- a baker saved 46% on the ingredients for their products without changing brands, received better terms, and now has both primary and secondary suppliers to make sure they're never left without inventory.

A larger client with $22M annual travel spend saved a total of $8M annually – over 36%. Innovate was able to do this without the client's staff having to change their travel habits (e.g. how far in advance they book, the hotels and airlines they use, etc.). They approached key airlines and hotels and created a bespoke mechanism for the client to consume services at pre-negotiated rates at their leisure.

To date, they have 100% client retention and 100% repeat business and you can see why.

Mark sees procurement as a strategic support function that aligns with your company's goals to help achieve the results you want. It's sourcing for value, not just price; better results in terms of services and products; better suppliers; and better overall value creation.

> **LESSON:** The right professional advice can help transform your business. Don't assume it's only for the big guys.

Chapter 8

To get the right answers you have to ask the right questions.

But it's impossible to ask the right questions if you don't understand what you could or should even be asking.

We all heard our parents say, "If they jumped off a cliff would you?" and most of us have learned to apply it pretty well in our personal lives. It's another story in our business lives, though, especially when it comes to transitioning a business into the digital age. All of a sudden we're back in middle school.

All too often business owners just jump off the cliff with their peers, following what they're doing in situations like deciding which SAAS (software as a service) to use for functions like email marketing, project management, or accounting, which platform to have their website developed on, what insurance to buy, or even whether they should hire employees.

Actually, when looking at services (especially digital) most never ask much about options because they don't even realize there are real differences between the options. They think "what's good for one is good for all" and usually just look at pricing. What they don't realize is that the people they're following didn't know the right questions to ask, either.

One example: a nonprofit client signed up for a multi-year commitment with a platform that provides donor management. Although they can take recurring donations they didn't realize the platform they chose didn't allow the donor to cancel it themselves, sign up for a total amount to give, or sign up for a specific number of payments. Instead, they have to contact the nonprofit who then has to cancel it. This is 2010's technology in a 2020's world, but it never occurred to the client to ask about these details. Recurring donations? Check. The devilish details? Oops, didn't think to ask.

To make matters worse, even if you work with a consultant many of them don't understand the idiosyncrasies of individual businesses enough to know to ask you the subtle questions that make all the difference. They know the products and software they're used to working with and that's all they think matters. My clients know I'm curious enough about details to often uncover questions they'd never think of.

LESSON: The devil is in the details. Find a trusted advisor who knows the right questions to ask so you can get the right answers.

"I'm a suit and tie guy"

When starting a new business, most of us probably just think about how much money we can make and the products and services we'll offer. While that's important, here's another reminder that the devil is in the details. I pound into clients that "you can't get the right answers if you don't ask the right questions, but the most important questions are the ones you don't even know need to be asked."

When you don't even consider basic things like what insurance will be required, the costs of purchasing and storing inventory, how many employees you'll need to hire, the types of employees you'll need, how sales will be generated, geographic constraints, the type of office or facility space required… The list goes on and on, and can be deadly to your business if you don't think about everything ahead of time.

Looking at just the question of what kind of employees you want to work with and how many, you shouldn't just think salaried vs. hourly, or full-time vs. part-time. You need to consider even the traits and personality types of those you would want to manage (and if you're even qualified to manage them).

Phyllis Pieri, CFE, has 30 years of experience helping match entrepreneurs with their perfect business opportunity and is known as *Your Franchise Coach*. She recalls working with a man whose neighbor had bought a residential cleaning franchise and was bragging about how great it was and how much money he was making.

Yes, it was a great franchise opportunity for the right person. This man was so focused on the money, though, that he hadn't even thought about the fact that he'd never worked with blue collar employees. He discovered he didn't enjoy working with them, but thankfully Phyllis helped him discover that before he got into a business that would have been totally wrong for him.

Phyllis says, "Sometimes people have the perception that 'anything is fine with me' and they're afraid they're going to miss something, but if you love what you're doing and are suited for it the money will follow."

Another example is a CPA who bought a glass company franchise. It was very profitable but after several years he decided he was ready to sell and wanted her help selling it. When she asked him why, he admitted that he didn't like working with contractors; it just wasn't his thing. He said, "I'm a suit and tie guy, and can't really relate to contractors."

Neither of these guys was a bad person, but they learned how important it was to consider not just how much money they'd make and how many employees they would have, but even the type of employees.

> **LESSON:** There's way more to starting a business than how much money you can make.

Know who wants what you have

Derek Hartley and Romaine Patterson were the hosts of Derek & Romaine on Sirius Satellite Radio from 2003 until 2015. An award-winning show targeting the LGBTQ community, they "welcomed an eclectic array of guests including Donald Trump, Martha Stewart, David Boudia, Joan Rivers, Samuel L. Jackson, and Rosie O'Donnell."

During the show's run they had started a cruise business that was growing at 40% annually. Derek said, "In my mind I was thinking this is a hedge against the future for us, that we can continue growing this cruise business and at some point it'll make enough money that, even if our show gets cancelled, it'll be fine. We'll just be two people who have cruises every year. What a terrible life that'll be!"

When the show was cancelled, neither knew what they wanted to do. They wanted to take a couple of months to figure things out "but had already planned to announce another cruise to Alaska. We had to make a decision: are we gonna keep doing cruises even though we don't have a show? Are we gonna keep our partnership going? We decided *let's announce this cruise and see what happens.* Even if we get other jobs the reality is it'll be some nice side money for us. We had a huge response and then had another cruise that Fall with even more people joining, and it really was the reason we decided to do our show on our own. We already had this other part of our business that was clearly alive." The show is now a paid subscription-based podcast.

They learned an essential lesson: "If you're going to have a business you have to know who you're reaching. Who's out there who wants what you have? And really figure out, *how can I deliver to this audience that I now know is there*? For us, we knew we had this core group."

Fred Seibert, MTV's first Creative Director had told Derek, "When somebody loves something they want a physical manifestation of it," so they created revenue streams from merchandise, too. They first started having bumper stickers, then added shirts and other merch related to the travel business and the podcast itself.

For example, on the first day of the podcast they sold a commemorative Day One shirt. With 1.5 million hits to the server it crashed, so they did a Day Two shirt with a 503 error message on it (the message a web server shows when service is unavailable). They also offer themed crates occasionally, like the *We Survived 2020* crate that included items like a 2020 dumpster fire T-shirt.

Derek says, "all of these pieces work together: people listen to the show, go on a cruise and meet other listeners, get a cruise shirt that they wear with their friends and post photos on social, people who don't listen to the show see it and ask about it and then they start going on cruises and meet everyone including me and Romaine, then they think *maybe I should listen to this show*, so they subscribe to the show and then buy more merch from the show. So all core parts of the business all loop into each other in a positive feedback loop."

LESSON: Knowing who wants what you have makes it easier to create multiple revenue streams from products and services they really want to buy.

There's power in choice

When we're feeling stuck, sometimes it's hard for us to see that choices are all around us. Emily Mishler is another who strongly believes that investing in your own personal growth will help you make better choices, and learn to make them with ease.

Founder of The Cultivated Group and author of the children's book series *Esmè the Curious Cat*, Emily says, "The synergy and the tandem growth that happens between personal and professional development, especially when it comes to owning your own business, is unlike anything I've ever seen. One grows, the other grows. Sometimes it's at the same time and sometimes there's a little lag time," but you can bet you'll see growth in both areas.

To make the best choices in your entrepreneurial and personal life, Emily says you need to "know yourself, serve yourself, and honor yourself, not from a place of ego or totally self-serving in nature but to make sure you have what you need to succeed."

Remember, there's no prescriptive formula for success. What you view as success won't be the same as what someone else views as success, yet we tend to make decisions based on some arbitrary definition of what success is or what we think others judge as being successful. That's a recipe for misery.

Emily is a big believer in taking the time to recognize the choices that surround you and making choices that allow you to make little tweaks as you go. She says, "It's about those compound little tweaks and those little decisions that really add up to make transformational changes over time. And time can be 3 weeks or time can be 45 years; it just depends on the scope of what you're truly trying to build."

LESSON: Make a conscious effort every day to recognize that you have choices, that things don't have to stay the way they are. Then make smart choices that let you make small tweaks that add up to big change.

From never working to CEO

Surely there's no way someone could go from never working outside the home to being CEO of a technology recruiting company, right?

Catherine Tanner wants you to know you're wrong.

From the beginning she and her husband, Tab Pierce, had agreed they wanted a traditional family where she would be a stay-at-home mom and he would be the breadwinner. It's not that they thought the alternative was bad, but Catherine's own mother was rarely around and she wanted a different upbringing for her own kids.

Things went great for decades and she was also the caregiver to her mother-in-law who lived with them. Then the kids grew up, her mother-in-law passed away, and Tab's cybersecurity business was in a crisis situation that he was battling. Not only was he consumed with turning it around, but things were so bad that he and Catherine were both driving for Uber just to be able to pay the bills. You'll read more about that in Chapter 12.

Since she was no longer a caregiver or raising kids, Catherine realized that she had a blank slate to create her future on. Their son had been running 3P&T Security Recruiting, a technology recruiting firm that he owned with Tab, for several years and Catherine decided to help him out part-time. She figured she could try to help grow that business and make some extra money herself.

She wasn't a seasoned recruiter, had no business background, and knew zero about the cybersecurity industry other than what she'd overheard Tab talking about over the years. She didn't even know the lingo, much less the technical terms, so she had a huge learning curve.

Her first potential client call was a referral and she had Tab sit in with her because she was so nervous. What if she didn't know the answer to a question? The thought of making a fool of herself was terrifying. "It was super hard," but Catherine discovered that it was also interesting and she really liked the work.

She ended up liking it so much, she and Tab bought out their son and Catherine is now the CEO of the company.

> **LESSON:** Having experience in a field isn't critical for becoming successful in it. Self-motivation, determination, and willingness and ability to learn are, though.

Buying a camera just makes you a camera owner

How many people do you know who buy a camera and then call themselves a photographer? Being able to point and click doesn't mean anything; if it did we'd all be photographers because of the cameras on our phones.

Marlana Semenza has decades of experience and her specialty is layering branding and strategic communication on top of photography. She doesn't just take photographs nor does she help create or develop a brand; she helps communicate your brand by capturing images that give insight into who you are.

She says, "Buying a camera makes you a camera owner, not a photographer. That doesn't mean you can't become one, but recognize where you are in the grand scheme of things." Her point is that you need to invest the time and energy it takes to become an expert in what you do and who you do it for.

Marlana disputes the belief that there's limited opportunity. She says, "That's absolutely untrue but you need to specialize! If you're not taking the time to specialize you're not great at anything."

Specializing doesn't just mean what you do, though; it also means who you do it for. There's plenty of business to go around if you figure out two things:

- what business you want, and
- how to communicate that to the right people.

But she warns that "knowing what you don't want to do and your no's are just as much or more important than what you want to do and your yeses."

Marlana's sweet spot is "helping clients break through to something bigger," but she only works with clients who already know the story they want to tell and who they want to tell it to. She knows exactly what she wants to do and who she wants to do it for. That's much different than "taking a picture" and requires a lot of research, understanding, and skill at messaging before the photography even begins.

> **LESSON:** To attract great clients and command higher prices, you must become an expert in your field AND define what you want to do, who you want to do it for, what you don't want to do, and who you don't want to do it for.

PART THREE - Thinking & Creating
Chapter 9

Daryl Hatton wanted to scratch his own itch but discovered that customers wanted a different itch scratched.

While coaching a lacrosse team, he couldn't get the guys to attend practice but they all magically showed up when he posted the practice schedule on Facebook. "So the question then was 'I wonder if I could post the fees and they'd all pay them' and that's how FundRazr was born. The idea was to make a business around that and see if we could make money off of helping others like me raise money for their sports team and maybe do fundraising."

Fee collection didn't go far but donation processing became quite popular with a lot of people. The problem was, Daryl and his team saw all of this activity but didn't really know what they were doing for a while. They knew the mechanics but not the impact.

"The sad part is we didn't know actually why they were coming," Daryl said. "They were showing up, they were demanding to come in, they really wanted this, but we hadn't done market research to say exactly why. We knew they needed money but didn't know their emotional motivation."

He says, "We did a screenprint of every campaign that had started, plastered the walls of the office, sat back and asked what's common about this? Why are people doing this? The purpose part of it didn't strike us because we were still trying to run it as a business. Then we got a Christmas card from a customer saying 'Thank you for helping save my daughter's life.' *What? How did that happen?*"

It turns out a couple had been living off the grid in Hawaii when their daughter was diagnosed with childhood leukemia and they didn't have health insurance. Since the father was a veteran, the military hospital in San Diego said they would take her but they had to get her there right away because childhood leukemia treatment has to start quickly to ensure survival. The parents raised $3500 for plane tickets and flew her over in the next couple of days. The doctor said "If they hadn't gotten there today or tomorrow she probably would have died."

Daryl told me, "Suddenly our net result went from raising money to solving problems and making an impact. That's the difference between building a better mousetrap and finding a problem to solve. I had this vision of a better mousetrap but it wasn't focused enough on what's the real problem I'm solving. I didn't have a focus on *what do they need us to solve?* but on *gee, I wonder if we can make this work?* We started with fee collections but people wanted to use it for fundraising. When we finally listened and started to do that, it started to go somewhere."

"It's one thing to say we helped buy some plane tickets, another thing to think about it in a different way. My daughter said, 'you have to humanize the result of whatever your product or service is. It's not about you helping them buy plane tickets. It's the emotional reason, what they did with the tickets." The parents were able to save the life of their little girl, and there's nothing more important than that.

> **LESSON:** Try to solve the customer's pain rather than trying to make them understand your product.

Collaborate to promote change

Stacey Burns-Fox has Certified Mastectomy Fitters who spend quality time with their mastectomy customers to ensure a proper, comfortable fit. This close work allows them to learn much about the effects of the procedure that surgeons are never in the position to see.

Stacey uses the knowledge gained in her business to speak to surgeons nationally about the reconstruction process, helping them understand how their surgical procedures affect healing. While she isn't a medical doctor, the more conversations she can have with them the more she can help educate them on the real life implications of decisions they make.

Surgeons were putting the drainage tube right where the bra band goes but had no clue it was a problem. Since it takes about a year to heal, placement where the bra puts pressure can be debilitating for women. Although that's an easy spot for the surgeon, Stacey was able to show them that moving it just an inch can mean a big difference in quality of life.

Her experience helped them help their patients. It's not that they didn't care but most surgeons are men and "that's just what they've always done, they've just never looked at it from another perspective."

Stacey says, "The way that works is communication: they're not experts in bras and I'm not an expert in their surgery, but if we can figure out a way together to be best for patients then that makes a huge difference."

Collaborating and learning from each other helps everyone and Stacey says, "Most collaboration is food for your soul. I feel good when people take my ideas and take my tidbits; that gives me fuel" to want to continue to learn and improve.

> **LESSON:** You can always learn from people who aren't experts in your field, and they can learn from you. Just a different perspective can often make 1+1 equal more than 2.

The magic & mystique of scarcity

Lots of marketers now talk about FOMO, or fear of missing out, but scarcity has always been a driving force in making people want something. That's why marketing with words like "limited time offer," "get it while it lasts," and "exclusive offer," works. It's also why adults fight in the aisles of retail establishments at Christmas to be one of the few who can get that year's hot item for their little darling, and might just be why you lose interest in your new flame when the thrill of the chase is gone.

This isn't a new phenomenon. The phrase "no one is a prophet in their own land" has its origins in the Bible, Luke 4:24, and basically means that we take for granted the things we're familiar with.

Adam White, the self-professed "Motown geek" you heard from earlier, grew up in England in the 60's. He said that when he heard Martha and the Vandellas sing Heat Wave the first time, "It was unlike anything I'd heard before, but just as important, it wasn't coming out of the place I lived in." Think about that last phrase… *"Just as important, it wasn't coming out of the place I lived in."*

Adam wanted something different, something rare that he had to search out, something all the other kids weren't listening to. While the music truly was great, that exclusivity naturally added to the excitement.

He continues, "In 1963, when I heard that record (Heat Wave), all British music fans cared about were the Beatles. I hated the Beatles. They were on television all the time or I could go down the street and see them in a local concert hall. There was no mystique or magic attached to them because of proximity. Detroit on the other hand, Martha and the Vandellas, thousands of miles away, the magic and mystique of something you can't get easily makes a real difference."

Hearing Adam say this himself with his British accent makes it much more interesting, though: lisakippsbrown.com/adam-white. *Sorry, Adam, I know I'm the one with the accent* :)

A prime example of scarcity marketing is McDonald's McRib sandwich, and an article on Inc.com by Nicole Carter sums it up perfectly:

"While McDonald's playing hard-to-get with the McRib certainly baffles most customers, from a business perspective, it has proven to be a wildly effective marketing strategy. The McRib's marketing strategy bundles the appeal of exclusivity, scarcity, and seasonality into one savory package. And it's become a strategy so successful that McDonald's is making the promotion perennial."

> **LESSON:** People love to be different or feel like they know or have something that others don't. Adding an air of scarcity, exclusivity, or limited availability to your marketing can work wonders.

Put on your 3D glasses

An idea person sees things differently than others. It's like wearing 3D glasses when everyone else isn't.

You can't buy those glasses, but you can earn them by thinking "what if" on a regular basis and allowing your mind to explore without fear. You may think you're not an idea person but I believe anyone can learn to come up with good ideas just by becoming more curious about your surroundings.

Make it a habit to ask questions like "what if?", "why?", and "why not?" Even if you don't ask them out loud, ask yourself mentally and reawaken the child in you, the kid who wondered about everything.

And here's something really cool: when you explore ideas and create opportunities with other people, it's like being able to see through those 3D glasses from different angles all at once. You're getting the viewpoints of other people, seeing things from angles that you never would on your own.

The magic of ideas is that one person's idea can actually generate another person's idea. The more you collaborate with other people, the more fleshed-out your ideas will become and the better you'll become at seeing things that others can't see.

> **LESSON:** Practice being curious: include the questions of why, why not, and what if on a regular basis to start seeing past what's obvious.

Winning the race to zero

It's common knowledge in business that you don't want to compete based on pricing because there will always be someone else who's willing to do it cheaper than you. It ends up being a race to the bottom, which nobody can win.

But what if there's a way you can win the race to zero? Daryl Hatton says there is.

He advises, "If you're in a situation where you're in a race to zero, who's going to be able to give it away for free first, the only way to win the game is to get there first. So don't go, 'We'll follow them down as slowly as we can.' Get creative about getting there ahead of time and getting to zero right away."

His trick for doing that? Find somebody else to pay for

it. "Your customer who you originally thought would pay becomes the user of the product or service, but there's somebody else who cares about them doing it. If you can get that somebody to pay for it you've got a competitive advantage. Now you can give it away for free and still make money."

His own crowdfunding platform, FundRazr, is the perfect example.

Everybody used to charge a processing fee of 5% for donations. Daryl says, "Then it became 4, then it became 3.5, and the race was on. So we said how could we actually do it to give it away completely for free? And the answer was to ask the donors to give us a tip to process the transaction."

They ask the donors to help them keep fundraising free for the charities they love by tipping.

"We're used to tipping in North America, anyway, so they're willing to pay the fee for the charity. Everybody gets to use our system completely for free and the donors are quite happy to make sure that it stays free for them. It was a higher value for them than it was for the charity."

In other words, charities would make the decision of choosing a platform based on cost; they would just go with the lowest fee. But donors make their decision to give based on emotions. Nobody is required to tip, but most people do because they know it helps their favorite causes be able to have free access to a great fundraising platform.

> **LESSON:** You can win the race to zero if you find someone else to pay for the product or service you're providing.

Rethink the traditional

I think it's very ironic that the education system is one of the industries that's the most entrenched in legacy thinking, but it also makes sense because most educators don't have experience in anything else. Sadly, students are being "taught" content that's already outdated and many of them know more about current topics than their teachers.

This isn't a new problem, though. You can refer back to Chapter 6 to read how Jeffrey Madoff was so frustrated in the 60's when his Political Science professor was teaching the same content he always had while a protest was raging right outside of the classroom window. There's also a very long list of successful entrepreneurs who quit college to pursue their dreams rather than stay in school to basically be trained to be middle managers.

What's worse now, though, is that young people think differently because their brains are wired differently and they're used to processing many things at once because of technology. The education system will literally be unable to teach them if they don't figure this out.

Enter Matthew Alex, founder of Beyond Academics, who says "universities have a herd mentality and aren't risk takers. They're going to become irrelevant unless they reform." The former Deloitte partner who led their Student Technology and Transformation practice is intent on disrupting the education industry.

If you don't believe universities are at risk of becoming irrelevant, just do a quick search on "companies that don't require a degree" and you'll find many examples ranging from technology companies to financial institutions. Even the Big Four accounting firms dropped the requirement for a degree years ago, with Ernst & Young saying years of research show "no evidence" that success in college translates to success on the job.

Matt says that people learn faster now and a course that used to take 16 weeks could take 2 weeks instead; there's no need to drag it out over those months just because it's always been done that way. He believes "students need to be in the classroom when having interactive, critical conversation, not when you're doing something that's structured. Unstructured learning needs more humans." He also believes that "books can be master classes."

To teach young people the way they learn now, he says "Universities need a learning platform that rivals Netflix or a gaming platform." They need to teach them the way they think.

Many adults also tend to continue their own independent learning much more now than they did decades ago; I know I learn something new every day. Matt says one way universities can reinvent themselves is to become "continuous learning ecosystems. Stop worrying about incoming freshmen; you should be worrying about how you can keep your alumni coming back."

During the time I was in college there was a push for as many people as possible to go to 4-year schools and those who went to community college were looked down upon as losers who couldn't get into a university. Decades later we started paying the price by not having enough welders, electricians, and others in skilled trades. Now workers in those trades can come out of school making $50,000 a year while too many of those with a Bachelor's degree chose a worthless field and have mountains of debt they can't pay off.

Between technology that's changing so rapidly that going to school can actually hold students back, expensive degrees that don't prepare graduates to be able to land a job where they can make a living wage, and the trades being in such high demand now, it's going to be really interesting to see how all this shakes out.

The industry is beyond ripe for Beyond Academics to disrupt it.

> **LESSON:** Look for areas where others have become complacent; they're ripe for disruption because everyone else is lazy or entrenched in legacy thinking.

Treat your ideas like the original art they are

Years ago I thought I wasn't creative at all because I thought of creativity as being strictly artistic. I couldn't paint or draw well, so how could I be creative?

It took many years for me to realize that people who can come up with great ideas are just as creative as artists. As a matter of fact, an idea person and an artist are really the same. They both come up with ideas in their mind that can then be brought to life so other people can see them.

An artist uses paint, brushes, pens, styluses, canvas and tablets to express their idea. An idea person's creation may be physical, like an invention that you can hold, but it can just as easily only be seen by the results that it generates.

And huge results can be generated when you start getting into areas like strategic partnerships. You can only see signs that they exist and you can't hold them, but they're there and they're powerful.

Ideas are like the inverse of black holes.

As black holes grow they suck in everything around them, never letting go (as far as we know!). As ideas grow, new things end up growing from them.

Elon Musk is one of the most innovative people of our time. He's a fountain of ideas and he isn't afraid to throw them out into the wild. He doesn't care if people think he's crazy.

The irony is that all the crazy ideas he throws out have the chance of creating an idea in someone else even if he never acts on them. It's like volunteer plants that grow from seeds in the wind! If that seed lands in just the right spot, it can grow into a mighty tree.

What might your ideas grow into?

> **LESSON:** Ideas are one of the most valuable things on earth; learn to view yours as such.

Chapter 10

Everybody thinks Richard Mulholland is a technology expert because he knows so much about using Zoom and PowerPoint.

You want to know his secret, though? He and his team just read the notes for every single update release.

Rich says, "Everybody got the same email from Zoom, and everybody got the same email from PowerPoint, but we're the only ones who read it. And then people are like, 'Oh my God, you guys are so on the cutting edge!' No, bro, we just read the email that you got."

It's funny that every one of us could easily do what he does but we're too lazy or busy. That's just fine with Rich, though. He says "lazy and busy, that's a beautiful combination" if you want to sell a service.

He told me he "realized in the world today nobody knew anything about online presenting. So I said to my entire team, 'guys, we have just got to become the experts. Nobody knows what they're doing. If everybody is a 2 out of 10 and we're a 3 out of 10, we're like kings!'"

You may recall that in Chapter 8 I talked about professional photography being much different than "taking a picture." and that may seem contradictory to Rich's statement above. But he also said, "Nobody knew anything about online presenting." Everybody thinks they know how to take a photo, so you need to put in more work to stand out.

Take it from Richard, "You want to narrow your area of authority. I don't know a lot about a ton of things, but I know a shit ton about presenting. So I'm not the technology guy. It sounds like I know a lot but I only know a lot about this very narrow area, which is presenting."

Word of warning, though: don't throw around industry jargon or what I call gobbledygook. A lot of people do that because they think it makes them look smarter and able to charge higher prices. You don't need clients to understand how to do the things you do for them but you do need them to understand what you can do for them.

I highly recommend following Rich on YouTube at http://getrich.af/youtube (and notice his memorable url that helps attract the right clients and repel others). His videos deliver tons of value and are very entertaining so you'll actually enjoy learning. He's great at simplifying communication, too, so you definitely won't be getting gobbledygook.

> **LESSON:** You can make a shit ton of money by knowing a shit ton about one thing that others are too lazy or busy to bother with.

Specialize to narrow the field

You know you're supposed to niche down rather than trying to be everything to everyone but have you done it? I bet not. It can be scary to do because you're afraid you'll miss out on a potential client, but it can also be hard to decide what you want your niche to be.

The reason it's so important, though, is because it makes it easier for your perfect clients to find you and for you to become known as an expert. Let's look at a couple of examples of specializing that aren't related to business to help you believe that it really does help.

I was a high school band geek and made All Regional Symphonic Band (the highest level of All Regional Band), but I know the only reason I made it was because I played bass clarinet. If I had tried out on the standard Bb clarinet I would have never made it because there was so much competition and I honestly wasn't that good. By trying out on a specialized instrument there were less people competing and I had a higher chance of making it.

Before Aaron Golub became the first legally blind

person to play NCAA Division I football, he didn't start out playing the long snapper position that he played in college. He had been playing football since he was a child, and in the 10th grade he played on the JV squad as a second or third string offensive and defensive lineman.

To have any chance of playing Division I college ball he needed to play first string on the varsity squad, but knew he'd never be able to do that as an offensive or defensive lineman. He decided to specialize and become a long snapper.

He spent hours and hours practicing, reached his goal of playing first string varsity, made the team at Tulane, and even went on to become an NFL free agent. While a free agent, he decided to leave football for the business world, though. He knew he had a much more realistic chance of becoming as successful as he wanted in business so once again adjusted his route.

Aaron says "I've always picked something I knew I could be good at, set a goal, and went after it. Although I've had to work ten times harder than anyone else, I do whatever it takes to get there."

It may take him longer to do something, but because he works ten times harder than others he can usually achieve his goals faster than they can. It's simple mathematics. If he's working while they're coasting, he's catching up and will end up passing them. You know, just like the tortoise and the hare.

> **LESSON:** Sometimes you need to adjust your route to achieve the level of success you want. Specializing is one way to do that: you'll end up with less competition, will stand out more, and can become the go-to expert.

Develop a niche that both you and your clients love

Before Kelvin Joseph started Kool Kel Marketing, he had been advising CEO's throughout his entire career, from working in the largest accounting firm to the world's largest marketing and advertising company. He has lots of great tips but when asked for his #1 tip for struggling businesses he replied without hesitation, "Make sure you have a real value proposition and a real target audience." That sounds so basic but that's why it's so important!

Kelvin says, "Stop being a jack of all trades trying to please everybody. Figure out who your target audience is, one that you can give tremendous value to, where what you're giving them is worth more to them than the money they're paying you. You can afford to do that because you're really specialized. People pay for expertise, not for general knowledge. You gotta have that one thing."

If you own a service business and don't know your

niche, Kelvin advises that you ask yourself what your customers are currently buying. He said, "The reality is, if you're in business, somebody is actually buying. You have to see if there are more people like them that could be a lookalike customer."

What if you're one of those people who's built your business based on doing what everyone else is doing, though? You're likely to have a problem: customers may be buying something you don't really want to be selling, even if you're making a lot of money doing it.

To really Disrupt Your Now, your niche needs to be something that people need and are willing to pay for AND that's worth it to you to offer. By "worth it" I don't mean just money. I mean whatever success means to YOU. If you're paid a fortune to do something that makes you miserable, it's just not worth it.

As Kelvin says, "Your business isn't going to be successful just because you make a lot of money. After you buy a house and, if you're into it, you buy a car that you like, there's not much else to buy. Wealthy people are giving away money. What are you working for? Anything you buy, after a week, it's normal to you. You can buy a new house and after a week it's a normal house. You buy a new car, after a week it's normal to you. You go on vacation, after a week you're ready to go home."

In fine-tuning your niche, there are two sides to look at: what's valuable to your client and what's valuable to you. If the client wants something that you're miserable or can't make a profit delivering and you decide to serve that niche anyway, you're setting yourself up for failure.

Let's take value to the client first: what can you deliver that's really valuable to them, the one benefit that strikes an emotional chord with them and pushes them to make the decision to work with you? Sometimes that's hard for us to recognize because we're thinking about "what we do" rather than "what we deliver."

If you're an accountant you might think, "I keep the most accurate books so clients don't have to worry about an audit." The benefit the customer might actually see, though, is freedom. They have many more hours to relax each week because they're not spending their time working "in" their business. A theoretical audit isn't top of mind for them whereas time is.

Now let's look at what's valuable to you: take a look at your best client and ask what actually makes them best. The answer to this question will depend on what's important to you, but I find common reasons include a combination of things like the amount of money they spend, the repeat business they provide, the fun and ease of working they bring to the relationship, the type of work you get to do for them, and the freedom they provide to do your best work.

The perfect niche for YOU, not the perfect niche for everyone else in your industry, is the one where you can deliver the highest value for the most money and fulfillment. The sweet spot is where value to the client and value to you align.

Once you've dialed in on that niche and developed messaging that's talking specifically to that one perfect client, it will be easier for you and them to recognize each other.

> **LESSON:** Finding the sweet spot where you can deliver the most value to your clients and get the most value yourself is key to developing a profitable niche.

"The author wins every time"

In 2004, Honorée Corder had written zero books. Now she's a Strategic Book Coach who's published more than 50 books with millions of dollars in sales, helped Hal Elrod expand *The Miracle Morning* book series, and worked with dozens of aspiring nonfiction authors to successfully craft, write, publish, launch, and market their books.

It all started with her meeting Mark Victor Hansen, co-creator of the *Chicken Soup for the Soul* book series, at a conference. "He asked what I did and I was very proud of myself and said *oh, I'm a coach and a speaker*, and did a little hair flip. He's like 'Yeah, that's nice. Everybody's a coach and a speaker. You better write a book,' " she recounted.

She recalls, "I had all those things go through my head that I think go through a lot of people's heads. Like, *who am I to write a book? What would I write about, who would want to read a book by me, what do I have to say?*"

Mark told her, "You need to have a book to differentiate yourself from the other people who do what you do, and if you have a message that you deliver..." She explains, "What he meant at that time was if you have a presentation you deliver that people like, turn that into your book. So that's exactly what I did. I asked a bunch more questions in that conversation and I took his advice to heart and then I acted on it and it changed my life."

She wasn't sure what to do while she was waiting for the books to be printed; remember, this was 2004, before social media campaigns. Marc Victor Hansen told her that when he and Jack Canfield were working to promote the original *Chicken Soup* book they did 7 things every day to promote it. So, Honorée went to her local newspaper and business journal and asked if they wanted to do a feature article. Then she called all of her contacts, told them she had a new book coming out, and asked if they wanted to buy between 10 and 100 copies. After she had success with that, "I started saying would you like to buy between 10 and 1000 copies, or 100 and 1000 copies, and sold 11,000 copies in three weeks!"

"It changed my career, it changed my business, it changed my trajectory, and it opened doors for me. It absolutely expanded my universe and every book since then has done the same thing," she said. In addition to selling the book for royalties, she used the book as a lead magnet to open doors, engage clients, and sell her business and executive coaching services.

"If there are two people that do exactly the same thing but one of them has a book and the other doesn't, guess what? The author wins every time," Honorée declares.

Think about it, most people can't even write enough to fill up a page. If you were to ask them to write something you'll most likely be met with a blank look; they wouldn't even know where to start. Contrasting that, you must have something to say if you can fill up a book, which demonstrates right out of the gate how different you are from your competitors.

After you write your book, you can also repurpose the content for online courses, speaking, and companion guides, creating more ways of engaging with clients and new revenue streams for years to come.

I asked Honorée what she sees as the biggest mistakes that self-published authors make. Her answers are:

- Having a bad cover (designing their own, using a cheap service or a premade cover, or not being on genre),

- Having a clever title that doesn't convey what the book is about,

- Not hiring a professional editor, and

- Not hiring a copywriter for the cover copy ("the cover copy shouldn't be in the voice of the author; it's meant to convert a sale in the ½ second you have for someone to choose").

LESSON: To truly differentiate yourself from competitors, write a well thought-out, professional book.

What's your polarizing brand trait?

A niche isn't just the products and services you offer and the clients you offer them to. It encompasses your entire brand, and by brand I don't mean your logo. I mean everything about you and your business, what people say and think about you when you're not in the room. It doesn't matter what you say about yourself if it doesn't jibe with the perception others have of you.

The most valuable part of your brand is anything that sets you apart from your competitors, even if some people see it as negative. You don't want or need everyone to like you, just the people you care about. If there's nothing to set you apart, you blend in. Nobody can find you or, even if they can, they don't recognize you as someone they're eager to work with because you're playing it safe.

Brooke Norman, founder of First6Media and author of *hey...you're muted: The Essential Post-COVID Marketing Handbook*, says "to create a galvanized following you have to be willing to be disliked. If you want to be top of mind, get very clear on whose cup of tea you are not because they're not yours either."

If you've been safely vanilla for a long time, Brooke advises that knowing "what your polarizing brand trait is, that would be a great place to start. Like, I can tell you that I have some pretty pointed opinions about what marketing is and what it's not. And if I alienate a group of people because it makes them feel like they waste their money, it also brings a lot of people that think *that's exactly what I think, too*, and those people find that worth spending money on."

I asked her for tips she would give to help you pull out your own polarizing brand trait and she gave some great ones:

She said "First, go back over the past month and think of the times you bit your tongue because you were like *it's not worth saying*. That is a polarizing opinion you have that you should stop and explore. Like, stop and think *what's not worth it?* Because now we're talking about what something's worth, which means there's a consequence for exposure. And those moments where you think there's a consequence for exposure, that's actually where to lean in and be like I don't agree with that or I have to ask you, when you said that did you mean this? You don't even have to reveal it. What you do have to do is start to be like 'we are not lackeys, afraid of you terminating us. We are always willing to break up with you and you should always be willing to break up with us.' "

If you're in a conversation and "you start to find yourself pulling back, write it down," she suggested. "You don't have to say it on the call but write it down and explore *what would I be willing to say*."

An exercise she has clients do is:

"Go through famous quotes that everyone loves. If you hate one that everyone loves, you should probably look into that. One of my clients had a visceral reaction to Einstein talking about 'intelligence isn't about this, it's about learning.' The client said if she could change Albert Einstein's quote she would... If you say, 'Albert Einstein said this but it should actually say that,' you have now said something worth listening to because people will disagree with that, which means there will be other people thinking like *finally, someone said it*."

On the topic of what people think about you when you're not in the room:

"If someone said, 'Oh my gosh, I just heard this other

client talking about you behind your back,' in good ways and bad ways, what do you think they said? What's wrong with your customer service and what do you hope people think about you? That's your brand, your commitment. How you want to be seen when you're not in the room is your best version of yourself. Like for myself, 'Brooke is no-nonsense, probably a little intense and dialed-in, talks too fast, but is sincerely invested in building an outcome that you're proud of.'"

LESSON: Being authentic in a way that turns off people you don't want to work with actually helps attract people you do want to work with because they recognize you as "one of them."

Chapter 11

The COVID pandemic created urgency in businesses throughout the world as they grappled with how to reposition themselves to survive.

Richard Mulholland needed something new FAST and didn't have time to mess around if he wanted to keep his business afloat. He says, "I allowed myself a half day of anxiety," but then he got to work.

In that critical time period, he felt that "brainstorming and surveying wasted time." Interestingly, he told his staff to ignore COVID updates and news because those were just distractions.

He wanted them to identify the unique problem that only they could solve *because* the pandemic happened, and to "stop trying to use tools to replicate how you did things" before the shutdown. He declared, "The job is not to replace, but to enhance" and that they should "ask, listen, diagnose, prescribe, over and over until they came up with an idea that worked."

The outcome of all these iterations was a new offering called Story-to-Stage. Rich was constantly on sales calls during the process and recorded all of the calls. He says, "I sold a product as though it was something we knew how to do," and his staff reviewed the recordings and rapidly iterated. They combined marketing, research, and product development all at once, and were able to get immediate feedback.

While most believe in research out the wazoo, Rich says, "The best research you can do is a sales meeting. If they buy, you've found a need; if they don't buy, you haven't."

His view is that researching by "asking people any question when their answer doesn't require them putting money behind it is not going to give you a real answer. If they say yes and give you the money, you know you've identified the dragon."

While running through these rapid iterations they didn't focus on any new clients because it would introduce friction. They went to current clients and clients they hadn't dealt with in a few months and brought them back into the fold.

Rich's original pitch was "Come and learn how to do this event" and he then offered a master class to answer questions. He was teaching them to do it themselves but most people don't really want to; they'd rather pay you to do it.

In Rich's words, "Lazy and busy, that's a beautiful combination!"

> **LESSON:** I can't say it better than Rich: "If they say yes and give you the money, you know you've identified the dragon."

Adapt existing products to meet new markets

Swiss-Mexican J. Roberto Inderbitzin, founder of REFRAME Design Studio based in Zurich, is a multi-disciplinary designer who sees technology as part of the ecosystem between people and innovation. He's worked with some of the world's leading brands and has been a member of the main jury of the Swiss Technology Awards.

Roberto knows you can't force every market to want your product. Various demographics and cultures value different features and may expect different pricing models. He uses the power of design to create products that exceed the requirements of the market, creating a competitive advantage for clients.

The Swiss company Wildbiene + Partner AG had an innovative product, the "Bee Home," that promoted safe pollination of food plants by non-stinging wild mason bees that can be kept as "pets" in the garden or on a balcony. It was being sold in Switzerland and they wanted to expand into German and French markets but those markets are much more price-sensitive. They knew the existing product wouldn't be marketable at their current pricing, but cutting the price of the existing product wasn't feasible.

They turned to Roberto to reframe their concept and he set about reimagining how they could change the assembly and materials to reduce the cost and make it easier to assemble, telling a story at the same time. The adapted product is injection molded but has wood in it and even smells like wood. He also reduced the assembly from a number of screws to 0 and eliminated the metal rods used in it, so it's actually easier to assemble than the original Bee Home. He said, "I enjoyed this project because it's a product with meaning, fun for the owner but helps the environment."

In reframing products, Roberto says, "I don't like to call it figuring out a problem; I like to call it figuring out a challenge. I let my mind go all over the place and like to freak out, like go way over the top and then go back."

He also creates his own unique products, like 3D printed facemask holders made with corn-based biodegradable Polylactic acid (PLA) and his own JR branded cufflinks at Jose-Roberto.com "for the man who wants to be different."

LESSON: You don't always have to create a new product; you can adapt existing products to meet a challenge or give them your own unique twist.

"Fun, nothing, this is a business model"

A few months after the COVID shutdown started, my friend Henry Sims posted a teaser of new personal branding photos of him on his motorcycle at the beach. The teaser was a really great photo and I was shocked to read that while he was at home in Los Angeles the photographer, Marlana Semenza, was in North Carolina! I had to get to the bottom of how that was possible.

Marlana says one of her friends saw a few people playing around with virtual photography on YouTube but they were all doing it for fun, something to distract them during the pandemic.

Knowing she had to find a way to keep her business moving forward, Marlana thought "Fun, nothing, this is a business model!" She played around with it to get consistent output and practiced with various friends and clients, especially beauty pageant contestants who are a big part of her clientele. All of this practice enabled her to experiment with lighting, iPhone versions, and other variables that would affect the quality.

Once she knew she could consistently deliver the professional quality she's known for, she created accessible pricing packages that made it "a no-brainer to get started."

In a profession that most would assume the pandemic would kill, Marlana has carved out a fun new offering that's opened her business to the entire world. From her home in North Carolina, she's photographed clients not only in the US but also in countries like Australia and Portugal. She got her first client through word of mouth and got the one in Australia through a mastermind group she's part of.

Marlana says, "The most difficult thing is teaching the client to be me."

> **LESSON:** People all around you are having fun doing things that could be turned into new business ideas.

Control and love your customer

In 2003 Samanta and Kelvin Joseph started a shoe business for a niche market, women who wear above size 10 and want to wear stylish, comfortable shoes. Serving this unmet market with beautifully designed shoes, they quickly turned $10,000 into a multimillion-dollar business and both made Inc. Magazine's inaugural 30 Under 30 list.

They initially built the business on B2B sales by selling to shoe stores. When the 2008 recession caused most brick and mortar shoe stores to close and online sales took over, though, they had to regroup. Developing a relationship with Amazon's Endless.com online store, Samanta Shoes became the #1 supplier for larger sizes. They were selling $100,000 worth of shoes to Amazon each month and things were great again. That's a lot of shoes!

Then Amazon bought Zappos, closed Endless.com, and began redirecting Endless.com customers to Amazon.com/Fashion. They said Samanta Shoes had to carry all sizes but when the smaller sizes didn't sell, Amazon shifted the blame to Samanta's. Kelvin pointed out, "They forced us to make them! When I'm selling size 6, 7, and 8 shoes, I'm competing with the whole world. But if I'm selling size 11, size 12, I got the best game in town, see? So I can compete with the big boys."

Samanta's Shoes had allowed Amazon to dictate the sizes because they had so much control over the business. All of their sales were coming from Amazon, but since that's not where people go to buy shoes Amazon quit ordering and Samanta's sales tanked. Crap.

The big lesson Samanta and Kelvin learned was that they needed to control the customer, not allow retailers to do so. In selling to shoe stores and then Amazon, they had forfeited the ability to build and connect with their own customer base.

"If you don't control and love your customer you don't control and love your business. When somebody else is responsible for the sales, they're basically running your company," Kelvin said. "The quality of clients and consistent, reliable revenue is your job to create if you want to have a successful business. If you're not working on improving the quality of your clients and establishing consistent, reliable revenue, then it's like a gamble."

Instead of closing the business, Kelvin went back to corporate America so Samanta could concentrate on rebuilding it. He jokingly said, "I don't know if my wife laid me off or if I quit but she said, 'This is Samanta's Shoes, not Kelvin's Shoes. You need to get a job.' Our kids were young and they didn't like eating Ramen noodles."

Samanta Joseph is now relaunching the business direct-to-consumer, building an exclusive community of women who have problems finding nice shoes in larger sizes. She's turned her customers' problem into a benefit: those shoppers are now the *only* ones who can get her beautiful shoes. Remember what we've said about exclusivity? Perfect game plan, Samanta!

> **LESSON:** If someone else controls your customers, they control your business and future.

Solve your own problem

After putting chemical relaxers in her hair to straighten it since she was 12 years old, Monifa Caines was done with the pain, scabs, and bald spots. She decided it was time to stop using those harsh chemicals, "Stop hurting myself, and love the hair that grows out of my head."

After letting her hair return to its natural texture, though, she had problems finding accessories that would work for her. To solve her problem she started making her own head wraps, head bands that were larger and could hold thicker hair, and hair combs with wider teeth. Friends started asking her to make some for them and it was fun and relaxing for her to do.

A military veteran, Monifa was working for a Fortune 500 investment bank headquartered in New York City. For a time she braided her hair and put it in a bun for work; when she later took the braids out, she washed her hair and slicked it back with gel. This led to a pivotal moment for her: a manager walked by her office and said "Oh, you took your braids out. Now you look professional."

That wasn't the worst comment, though. At one point she was told to go across the street to Duane Reed and buy a box of straightener to put in her hair at lunchtime, and was even told she wouldn't be promoted because of it. Monifa was devastated. She thought, *I can't even do something that is cultural or wear the hair that grows out of my head. They don't want to see it. They don't think it looks good.*

Not long after that she suddenly became seriously ill and was left unable to work. A native New Yorker, she could no longer afford to live there and moved back into a home she'd bought in Las Vegas while in the military. It took her about 5 years to recover, which gave her plenty of time to think about how she could take charge of her life and do what she wants to do. That's when she realized she was going to start her own business. It was the genesis of her company, Queen of Spades Style, through which she sells accessories she designs and has crafted by women artisans in countries around the world.

Monifa was recently selected to participate in The Workshop at Macy's, the world's first and most "exclusive retail-vendor development program designed to give select high potential diverse, LGBTQ, veteran and women-owned businesses the tools to better succeed and sustain growth in the retail industry."

She's doing what she loves, building a business she's proud of, and helping develop woman-owned businesses throughout the world. That's much more fulfilling than being stuck working for a Fortune 500 company!

> **LESSON:** Your future might just lie in solving a problem that's personally important to you.

Or, get close to a problem you want to solve

Sometimes you want to solve a problem that, unlike Monifa's, isn't your own problem and you may not know a lot about it. What then?

Todd Connor has some practical advice for you. He's founder of Bunker Labs, a nonprofit that's helped hundreds of military veterans launch and grow businesses, author of the book *Third Shift Entrepreneur,* and has been in the trenches with business types from solopreneurs to companies that want to scale. Todd has seen almost every mistake imaginable. His advice is, "Get close to the problem you want to solve or the business you want to launch."

When you want to add new services to an existing business or start a new business in an area that you're not very experienced in yet, this is a great way to learn without taking on the risk.

For example, he advises, "If you work in accounting but dream of owning a restaurant, go work in a restaurant and design your own internship. Don't go get a degree. Figure out what they're doing right and wrong, what their business model is, how they market, what they charge, what their customers say, and who their customers are."

By the way, Kelvin Joseph actually did this exact thing when he left Samanta's Shoes. He went to work for the CEO of Saks Fifth Avenue and did strategy work and internal audits to lower expenses. He said, "I'm selling luxury shoes as my family business so why not get a job working for the biggest luxury retailer in the world at the time?" He did that for three years and gained valuable experience that will help grow Samanta's in this next phase.

Another piece of advice from Todd is his mantra "quitting isn't starting." He means you shouldn't quit your job or current business to try out something new. He advises that you start today (you know, like *Now*) by doing things like research and planning. To test how it goes before you go all-in, you can try a popup shop; even large companies use popup shops to test new concepts, so why not you?

Easing in gives you a way to do it on the side to get your feet wet, and to even try various ideas before committing. What you don't want to do is make a mistake like Phyllis saw in an earlier chapter, where a franchise owner realized he didn't even like working with the type of people who are naturally in the industry he bought into.

> **LESSON:** Take time to research and ease into doing something new rather than jumping in all at once. You'll be more prepared if you decide to go with it, but will also be saved from making a bad decision if you find it's not for you.

Start with something ugly and cheap

Blake Hogan, the CEO of Bunker Labs, advises entrepreneurs to "Move forward based on evidence, get something super cheap, super ugly, and see if people who aren't your Mom will give you money for it. Take your thing to the real world for feedback to put back into the loop, and ask yourself, *do I have an idea worth pursuing and do I want to pursue entrepreneurship?*"

He knows this is best because he did the exact opposite in his first business, and (kinda) jokingly says, "I didn't go to Harvard but I paid for it." He and his partners started Vet Commander to help veterans and employers match up for hiring. Their goal was to develop a SaaS (software as a service) that they would then license to job boards.

"We built a very big piece of software before we brought it out for the world to see, a very expensive piece of software. We put it in front of folks like Indeed and others and they were like 'We kinda like it. Do you think you could make it do this and do you think you could make it do that? Me, not being an engineer, I went *yeah, of course, no problem*! I went back to the team and said can we do this and they're like *are you outta your damn mind? That's another 6 months, that's another $100,000!*"

Blake says they didn't ask enough questions up front so they could build something clients would be willing to pay for. "We could have tested it for free with Facetime, Skype or Powerpoint" instead of developing the software first. Free is good.

Contrast that with his next venture, BreakAway Safety Solutions, which "we really did out of a civic purpose at first. Shortly after the shooting happened in Las Vegas the CMA Fest was going to happen in Nashville and the city and others were worried about how to make it safe."

Blake and a group of veterans, entrepreneurs, and artists got together and "all these folks were saying, 'well what about countersnipers, what about a Kevlar blimp?' And the Marine in me was like, *why don't we just make it easy for people to get outta here? Why don't we just build a breakaway gate?*

They weren't sure how it could be built but decided to give it a shot. "We built a 1x1 model out of a little popup banner and then we built a giant one out of pieces of fence and we just kept iterating on it until we found something that would work for them."

"We didn't have any industry experience and we had no industry relationships, so we couldn't fake it. We were so honest and were just like, *how do you want to get this? Who do you want to get it from? How much do you want to pay for it? How do you want to pay for it?* So it was all these much more open-ended questions."

That process led to a solution, "a 10' gate. It's two 5' sections with bases that can fit in the back of a pickup truck, can be set up by one person in under 15 minutes, and it's less than $10 a foot. So, within a couple of months we built a product and put it on the CMA."

Due to weather conditions at that very first event, they had to evacuate over 20,000 people and were able to do it "in a matter of a few minutes." Amazing!

Contrasting this with his first business, Blake points out, "There was a bigger mission here. We weren't actually even thinking about this as a business. The reason we turned it into a business was, at the event some folks from the Chicago Marathon said, 'How do we get this in Chicago?' So, just off the cuff, I said *well, we have a licensing agreement and we can license it*. Then we had to figure out how to put together a licensing agreement and we protected the Chicago Marathon. We've now gone on to safely evacuate 150k+ fans, protect 2M+ fans, and have a patent pending product." Brilliant!

LESSON: Asking a lot of questions up front and doing quick and dirty iterations to get customer feedback is the best way to decide if an idea is even worth pursuing.

PART FOUR - Starting & Doing

Chapter 12

Focus your efforts on things that support your long term goals.

Tab Pierce is rocking it but it hasn't always been that way.

Author of *Upsurge: Wreckage to Triumph, Rebuilding Your Personal and Business Life* and founder of Caliber Security Partners and his new business Refiners, Tab's life and business were in shambles not very long ago.

He founded Caliber in 2010, providing cyber security services to enterprise clients and emerging technology companies. Although he had years of fruitful business growth, including two acquisitions, a few poor business decisions threatened both his business and family. Stress took its toll and he fell into deep depression, constantly doubting himself and fearing what might be next.

Everyone gave him the same advice: close the doors and walk away. But to Tab, closing the doors wasn't an option. He owed the IRS hundreds of thousands of dollars and he knew the only way he would ever be able to pay it off was to turn his business around. The IRS doesn't just go away, and no job would generate the type of income needed to overcome that massive debt. Over the next several years Tab's single goal was to turn around his business and personal life but he knew he had to take it in manageable chunks.

He says, "I had a good plan that spanned out far but I really wanted to make sure that I did the day well. I just wanted to do THE DAY, not tomorrow, just that day. I would tell myself, *tonight I'm gonna put my head on the pillow and I'm gonna look back and I'm gonna say whether or not things went the way I wanted them to go, I did everything I said I was gonna do.* So I leveled up, I did my part. Now, there are things outside of my control, can't control that, but I'm gonna do my part really well."

Tab and his family made many sacrifices, with even him and his wife driving for Uber just to be able to pay the bills, but they made it. Now he uses the lessons he learned from his mistakes to help others avoid the agony they went through. He wrote *Upsurge* to share his story and started the Refiners community to help business owners and professionals who want to improve their business and personal performance.

LESSON: Following through on a daily plan that focuses your efforts and supports your long term goals gives you more control over reaching those goals successfully.

Work on your business instead of in it

It seems like one of the biggest struggles for entrepreneurs is learning to work on the business instead of in the business. We get so engrossed in making sure we can meet short term needs like cash flow or catering to an important client, we often put our nose to the grindstone and before we know it days, weeks, or months have passed by.

What looked like a good idea turns out to be terrible. We're now further behind in reaching our long term goals and often we've just amplified the short term needs we were trying to solve.

When Matt Deutschman went to Croatia for his honeymoon, he was still having to work several hours a day in his promotional products business, Doubletake Promotional Marketing, and dealing with the time difference in communicating with clients. He realized he was a slave to his own business and thought *what's the use in owning a business if I can't take off for my own honeymoon?*

Then a couple of other events brought that thought into even greater focus:

- He and his wife found out they were going to have a baby and he knew he needed to make big changes to be able to spend as much time as possible with his family.

- They moved to Chicago for his wife's job and he was terrified he would lose all of his clients because he had set it up so people did business with Matt Deutschman, not Doubletake Promotional Marketing.

Matt began working on setting up "the Doubletake way" of doing things rather than Matt Deutschman's way. He needed to document everything he did in the business and create processes that could be replicated.

This document became the Doubletake Process Manual, a training resource for new hires. It's an organic step-by-step process for doing everything in the company and is constantly updated.

Matt admits he wasn't the greatest at letting go of control but developing systems and hiring great people has given him the foundation to do that. He says, "I used to think I would have to be okay with someone who could only do 80% of what I could. Now I'm perfectly fine knowing that members of my team can do things better than me."

He has realized that the key to real growth is finding people with complementary strengths, which frees him up to do strategic planning.

> **LESSON:** Working on the business instead of in the business gives you much more freedom and lets you build a more valuable business that you may someday be able to sell.

Don't build your business on someone else's

When Daryl Hatton's team first developed FundRazr it was all on Facebook, an innovation that could run within the Facebook newsfeed. Users could make a contribution from within Facebook but it was FundRazr's software. "We were one of the very few companies in the world that were ever able to develop the capability. Then Facebook messed with our future two ways," Daryl said.

Within the first year, Facebook made changes to the interface that had allowed companies to connect with the Facebook system. Daryl says "that wiped out everything we'd been able to invest in. We had to start again from scratch but now with no funding."

"Meanwhile, Paypal was having troubles of their own trying to make their apps work on social media. They recognized that FundRazr was nimble and we were usually able to fix our software quickly when Facebook broke it," Daryl said. "After we were killed off by Facebook the first time, fortunately PayPal offered to help us build the next version of FundRazr and also help market it for us. They said we could keep the product; they just needed a better way for their customers to be able to fundraise using Facebook."

Daryl's team had to deal with Facebook making changes that broke their software weekly, though. "Every

Wednesday was horrid. We'd just kind of sit back and hold on and go *what's gonna happen today?* Then some engineer at Facebook would throw a switch, something would break, and we'd quickly scramble and try to fix it," he remembered.

A few years later, Facebook struck again when the company decided to give away fundraising for free. Daryl says they knew that was coming, though, and were already working on the next version of FundRazr; they built it to run on their own independent platform rather than building it to run on Facebook any more.

Daryl warns strongly against building your business on top of any other business. "Any day they can change the rules or pull the switch, and you don't want them to have control over your future. It's too convenient. For a long time you could get people to your Facebook page because it was growing organically and people forgot how to market their own products. Then Facebook said 'Oh, if you want to get to this audience now you have to pay for our ads.' Now it's a tax, it's the Facebook tax on your business. Google does the same thing. How much do you have to spend on customer acquisition with Google? It's the Google tax."

Don't be fooled into thinking this warning is only for technology companies, though. If you're relying heavily on social media platforms to build any business you'll always be at risk of them changing the rules on a whim.

I'm not saying don't use them, but be smart about how you're relying on them and don't let them control your customers.

The only digital contact list you truly own is your email list, so you must make building that list a high priority. With your own email list, you can always reach your contacts independently of any other platform. I also recommend backing it up regularly so you don't run the risk of losing it in the event of some type of catastrophic system failure.

I would also be wary of building your business in a way that relies too heavily on affiliate income or any other company's products or services. You could invest years developing a specialty in a certain service or brand, only for it to close shop.

This even applies to brick and mortar companies: always have backup suppliers in the event a company goes under.

Remember what happened to Samanta's Shoes in the last chapter? Amazon held the keys to their customers and dictated their business in a way that almost killed it.

LESSON: Relying on other businesses too much for the operation of your own lets them control your future.

Do what you're good at and delegate the rest

Bill Bloom, founder of Bloom Financial and author of *Retire as You Desire*, has a passion for helping those 50 and older be ready to retire because of something he saw as a child: the Dad of one of his friends died young and had no savings or insurance, making the loss even greater for the family. Seeing that loss made him want to help make sure people don't run out of money so they can "retire as they desire," with a purpose and passion so they'll want to continue to learn and grow.

When most people hear the term "wantrepreneur" they think of someone who wants to be an entrepreneur but never actually acts on it. Bill looks at it in a much different way, though. He thinks of a wantrepreneur as "someone who wants to do too much or who is doing too much" so they're never able to reach their potential.

Everyone is probably really good at only two to three things maximum and Bill believes that wantrepreneurs "never find the people who can help you and take things off of your plate." He says the key to breaking past that is to focus on "those few things that you're really, really good at, the things that give you energy and that fire to get up out of bed and go change the world and go help people, and have a team around you to do all the other things that you're not good at."

In his own business, Bill hires around his strengths and hires others for their strengths, "what they're really good at and love doing." Doing so not only allows him to concentrate on the parts of his business that he enjoys and is best at, it also allows those he hires to be happier and more fulfilled because they're able to experience the success that comes from using their own strengths.

Bill also takes "who not how" a step further, though, by applying it to his acceptance of clients. He knows that working with the wrong clients is just another way of doing too much and only works "with grateful people, the right fit clients; there's someone else out there for the others." Like Kerry says in Chapter 5, it's okay say no.

> **LESSON:** Figure out the two or three things that you're best at and enjoy the most, delegate everything else, and only work with the clients who are a good fit for you.

Envision what you want and plan backwards

Evan Guzman always knew he wanted to be an entrepreneur but also knew he wasn't ready early in his career, recognizing that he needed more experience. So how could he get entrepreneurial experience before he was an entrepreneur?

His approach was to bring an entrepreneurial mindset to

every job he had. He took the time to understand himself, pretended the job was his own business, and treated it as an agency within an agency. Whether you're an employee who wants to become an entrepreneur, or an entrepreneur who wants to break into a new area, you can learn from Evan's approach.

He was drawn to doing something worthy and decided to take the job as Director of Talent Acquisitions for the American Cancer Society, where he spent ten years creating and building their Diversity & Inclusion program. Recognizing that veterans are a rich source of talent and have great experience in teamwork but often struggle to find a job after leaving the service, he made hiring them a primary focus.

When he later learned that Verizon was looking to hire a Global Head of Military Programs and Engagement to create, develop, and run their new initiative, he knew this was a perfect fit for him to build on the experience he had gained at ACS.

He didn't go into the interview with a resume like everyone else, though. He created a PowerPoint presentation to differentiate himself, showing he understood the needs of the military community and the skills they bring to the table. He was applying for a job but pitched like an entrepreneur. It's no surprise that Verizon saw the potential and hired him.

The position gave him the opportunity to make even more of an impact in his mission to hire veterans, and he led and managed high level public and private sector partnerships to help veterans get meaningful jobs in the civilian world. He also provided every living Medal of Honor recipient and their spouses with a free phone for life.

Evan's strategic approach led to many awards and helped Verizon be recognized as best in class for their veteran initiatives. When the company got to the #1 spot in Best for Vets, it led to an impressed shareholder emailing the COO who then emailed Evan, saying he never gets emails from shareholders talking about how great they're doing. He wanted to know more. Suddenly Evan was talking shareholder value with leadership, a giant leap from the average person working in Diversity & Inclusion.

He now had great experience under his belt and was able to leave Verizon on a high note, confident that he could be a successful entrepreneur. He started The MilBrand Project, a unique agency dedicated to helping companies attract and retain veterans and military spouses, better engage with the military community, and work with veteran owned startups.

If you're serious about engaging with the military community in meaningful ways, not just paying lip service, there's nobody better to work with than Evan.

And then, since 25% of active duty are NASCAR fans and 18% of NASCAR fans are veterans, you can come and partner with our NASCAR team that races to combat veteran suicide to round out your strategy! There's more about that mission in the final chapter.

> **LESSON:** When you can envision what you want, you can reverse engineer to understand what you need to do to get there and when you need to do it.

Results are a reflection of process

Too many people wonder why they're not getting better results and are too quick to blame others instead of themselves. Aaron Golub says the answer is simple: "Your results are a reflection of your process."

He's a big believer in time management and says that "Success is simple if you stick to a process and routine and work harder than everyone else. Be creative, work hard, check off your boxes."

Aaron micro-chunks his days, creating blocks of time to make sure he gets everything done that he needs to do. He also has what he calls "daily business non-negotiables," things that absolutely must be done regardless of what might pop up.

If you're tired of not getting the results you want, it's time to choose success over bad habits. Aaron says, "brains are wired to want to do what's easy but it takes just as much effort to make the decision to touch the snooze button as to say I'm gonna get up and work out."

The problem is that it's hard to switch patterns, though. That's why most people fail at sticking with New Year's resolutions, diets, and workout programs; they try to do too much at once and the mind rebels. If you really want to change, it's easier to make small changes over time.

Let your mind and body get used to one change, allowing it to become habit, before you bombard it with another. For example, if you want to start your day earlier don't suddenly set your alarm to go off two hours earlier. Set it 15 minutes earlier for a week or two and then increase by another 15 minutes until you're rising at the time you want.

Aaron advises that "as soon as you hear the voice in your head say 'I don't want to do this,' that's exactly when you need to do what it is you're trying to procrastinate. That's how you rewire your brain."

LESSON: It's important to create processes that work for you, but don't try to do everything at once.

Chapter 13

Being a filmmaker, Dr. Greg S. Reid decided he wanted to see what it's like behind the scenes "as one of the cattle call people."

Already an entrepreneur, film producer, keynote speaker, and award-winning author of numerous books including *Stickability: The Power of Perseverance* and *Three Feet From Gold*, he applied to be an extra on the long-running TV show Ghost Adventures and was selected for a part.

After finishing all his scenes around midnight, he was hanging around talking with other cast members. Soon after that Greg was on my live show and shared, "They're going to class learning acting, getting agents, doing all this stuff, and I said, 'You're not gonna believe this but I'm kinda like Undercover Boss – I actually make movies and TV shows and I just wanted to see what it's like on this side. In fact, I'm getting ready to do a couple of shows.' Not one person asked me to be in my show, and these are people giving their whole time, life... and I'm literally sitting there saying I'm looking for…"

The frustration on Greg's face was palpable as he shared the story. He said, "I just went *that summarizes most of America; most people let their big but keep them from what they want – not the one they're sitting on*. They go, 'I'd go do that, too, but…'"

It's amazing that so many are willing to spend countless hours and dollars supposedly in pursuit of their dream, but they never take decisive action to be in control of their own future. That's really just another way of procrastinating and, in my opinion, is rooted in fear of failure. It's easy to do the busy work but hard to step out of your comfort zone.

> **LESSON:** Opportunity surrounds you, but it's up to you to get off your big BUT and take action to seize it. Nobody is going to chase you down and beg you to act.

Don't be a crab on the beach

If you're expecting advice, feedback, or support from others, just make sure you know who to listen to and who to ignore. Most people are terrified at the thought of the risks that we entrepreneurs take and we can't imagine how boring life would be by not taking them. Your family and friends love you and want the best for you but you can't expect them to give you good entrepreneurial advice because you're thinking like an alien to them. Seriously.

Daryl Hatton says, "You need to have the ability to look foolish or look like you're insane for a little while because all you're doing is looking ahead where people aren't willing to look. That scares people and they want to pull you back, because what happens if you're actually successful and escape?" It's kind of like when friends or family sabotage a diet or workout plan because they're afraid you'll look too good, not that they'd ever admit it.

He told me about seeing fishermen in Mexico who throw crabs in a pile on the beach when they catch them. He said, "The crabs hold each other in the pile because leaving is *dangerous*." If a crab were to leave the pile it could get back in the water and save itself, but they all stay in the pile because it feels safe. Then they're eaten. Oops.

Everyone around you wants to hold you in that safe pile. Don't let them! Climb out, get back in the ocean and save yourself. (*Learn more about "crab mentality" at wikipedia.org/wiki/Crab_mentality*.)

Early in the days of FundRazr people would say to him, "Facebook? You mean the thing all the kids are playing with? You're going to build a business around that? Give me a break!" They had no clue of the possibilities because they didn't have the imagination to understand what Facebook could be. Daryl says "you have to learn to balance out *that was an interesting piece of feedback but it's not the truth*."

> **LESSON:** Learn to tune out advice from the middle-of-the-bell-curve people without vision who can't understand why you don't just play it safe.

Follow your dreams

Air Force veteran and reservist Charlynda Scales grew up eating a sauce that her grandfather had created, one that he used at all meals and never shared the secret recipe for. Eight years after he passed away, her mother revealed that Charlynda had inherited his secret sauce recipe in his handwriting, the only copy of the recipe.

Being the eighth in line, she didn't understand why she was the one it was left to but thought to herself, *is it just a piece of paper or is there something more to it*? She decided, *there's something more to it; I know it, it's got to be*.

Charlynda said, "I just kind of waited for something to manifest, there's more here... and I had a dream, it's so cliche, but I did." In her dream there was the country store she knew as a child, and "I walked into this store and there was nothing in the store except bottles of this red sauce with his face on it. And I was like, *that is what I'm gonna do. I have to do this, I'm gonna bottle it.* But I don't know how."

When she got up she searched for "free help" and one of the sites listed was SCORE. Their site said "make an appointment with your local chapter for free mentorship." At the meeting they said she could make it a bottled retail product, and Charlynda said "I don't know what retail product is, so you gotta break down all of the vocabulary for me because I don't know what you're talking about. They started with me from scratch, Business 101, Food 101."

Charlynda's grandfather served in the Air Force during the Korean and Vietnam War, where his call sign was "Mutt" because he fit in everywhere, so she branded the product Mutt's Sauce in his honor and put his photo on the label.

On the advice of her mentor, she started out selling locally at farmers markets and independently owned grocery stores to test it out and refine her skills. That gave her a chance to learn about sales and marketing on a small scale without hurting her business. "People are forgiving; *oh, she's new, bless her heart*." She also joined her local Chamber, which threw a launch event for her; she had 700 bottles made for it, sold every one, and used the money to make more sauce.

At the 6-month mark she went to the Black Enterprise Entrepreneur Conference "just to soak in information." They had a pitch contest where they were going to pick the top 10. Charlynda says, "In my arrogance and my non-humility, which I had been told all my life by my grandfather that humility would take me further than money, all I was thinking was *I am good, and I'm gonna get this money!*" WRONG. She didn't make the top 10. "I was like, *forget this, man.* I left the building and was gonna go get a margarita."

She had taken her graphic designer with her and he told her how wrong she was. "It's not about you. You should be in there supporting the ten who did get chosen." Realizing he was right, they returned to the building and as soon as they entered people were yelling, "Charlynda, run! Run to the stage!"

"So, I'm running; I dropped everything I had in my hands, took my heels off and was running to the stage, for what reason I didn't even know what. But when I got there huffing and puffing they said the next three people who made it to the stage were going to get one minute to pitch in front of the panel. I got to the stage and I tell you, it felt like an out-of-body experience. I was just pitching for my life."

As she was leaving the stage there was a lady standing there who asked if she knew who she was. "Now you know you're important when the first thing you ask is, "do you know who I am?" and I felt bad because I was like, *no*. But I learned that she was a behemoth in the food and beverage industry. She said, "What you need to do right now is go down the hall. There's a lady handing out badges and I think she's about done. Do you know that Shark Tank is in this building? You need to go right now!" So I was like, again, dropping everything..." Charlynda found the lady as she was actually walking out the door, and managed to get bracelet number 500, which gave her 1 minute to pitch.

To get the full effect, you really need to listen to her tell this story herself: lisakippsbrown.com/charlynda.

Over the next four months she made it from the local level to the national Shark Tank but you have to wait until Chapter 14 to find out what happened next...

> **LESSON:** Sometimes dreams really are trying to send you a message.

Diversifying is a lifeline

Kelvin Joseph started out in the financial world, and just before he started Kool Kel Marketing he was CFO for Steiner Sports where he worked his way up to second in command as COO and CMO. He told me, "The thing that pushed me to move from having a financial background to having a more sales and marketing background was that when I was CFO there, the company was owned by Omnicom. That's like the biggest marketing and advertising company in the world so there was a lot of pressure to increase sales and revenue. I went in thinking I was doing a good job as

CFO and asked for a raise. The CEO said to me 'You're the highest paid person that don't make no sales!' That's when the bell rang in my head that at a company you are either a revenue driver or you are an expense, and the more expensive you get the less valuable you are. Because value is the difference between what you pay and what you get. The beautiful thing is, that's when I pushed myself to build my own division at that company." He built it from scratch, growing it to a $10,000,000 division where he connected large companies like Morgan Stanley and Oracle with athletes for endorsement and events.

Kelvin figured out "I was always a relationship guy so that was my way of selling. I wasn't going to sell merchandise; that wasn't really what I wanted to do, but I was able to build the corporate relationships. That led me to say *wait a second... If I can build a $10,000,000 division for Omnicom, I can start my own marketing business*. The next thing you know I created Kool Kel Marketing. I was Kool Kel in high school so I just said *listen, I can be Kool Kel again*."

He had a one-year non-compete when he left Omnicom so he began to advise companies based on his background of advising CEO's throughout his career. First he advised store owners, then executives at Amazon in the shoe division, and the CEO's of Saks Fifth Avenue and Steiner, among others.

Kel said that "every company can't afford to have Magic Johnson at an event, but while I had my non-compete I realized these companies still had to grow their sales and they need to build relationships." He was doing a lot of events, strategic introductions, helping companies get their marketing strategy on one sheet of paper and develop a more focused target audience. Having the non-compete forced him to expand his knowledge and become more solid in that fundamental area. "I had a beautiful first year even with one hand behind my back with a non-compete. It was glorious!" he exclaimed.

When the non-compete ended things really started taking off, with lots of events with the biggest companies and most famous athletes in the world. Then the pandemic hit.

Kel says, "I had to cancel about $600,000 in events. For the first several weeks of the pandemic, I'm not ashamed to admit I was down, I was depressed. I didn't get out of bed for like three weeks. I didn't leave the house and I wasn't leaving the bed!"

The non-compete had been a blessing in disguise, though, because it had forced him to help businesses grow their sales, "and what do businesses need now? They don't need to do a big event, they just need me! That's why I started increasing my social media content so I could be more known as an expert in marketing instead of an expert in sports marketing."

He expanded his target market, too. "Instead of only being able to talk to the top companies that can afford to have a big name athlete at an event, which was a limited target audience, the world kind of opened up for me because what small or mid-size business doesn't need help right now? The big companies wanted me for my sports knowledge and the small companies wanted me for my brain."

Kelvin's story is chock full of disruption at every turn! Transitioning from finance to sales and marketing, the Samanta Shoes story in Chapter 11, launching his business, working around the noncompete, dealing with the shutdown... Lots of twists and turns but he just keeps winning.

LESSON: Diversifying gives you more tools to withstand volatility and meeting challenges head-on gives you an invaluable opportunity to learn and grow.

BONUS LESSON: Even Kool Kel was depressed when the pandemic hit. Now you can stop feeling guilty.

Perfection means you never took off

Brandon Straza's high school algebra teacher told him he wouldn't make anything of himself, that he wasn't meant for college. With a brother who was class salutatorian and sister who was a top 3 golfer in the world in high school, that comment was just the motivation he needed to prove the teacher wrong.

He did go to college and got a degree in finance; like me with my accounting degree, though, he didn't enjoy it. He started thinking about starting an insurance company and all of his family warned him not to do it. "Get a job, do something stable."

A man he looked up to said otherwise, telling him "Most people in our industry are lazy and stupid so it doesn't take much to succeed." So Brandon started his business.

Over 8,000 clients and 7-figure annual revenues later, he felt like he was doing something anyone could do, though, and didn't feel a purpose. That's when he decided to create The Naked Agent to interview mortgage lenders and realtors.

Leading with the give mentality, he would video the interviews and buy ad space to put them in front of another audience but wasn't going to charge those he interviewed. All of the advice he got was along the lines of, "Do not go do this. This makes no sense whatsoever." Brandon's response: "Ok, sounds good!"

He contacted a guy he wanted to hire to work with him, saying "Here's my idea. Here's what I'm going to do, but I need you and your family to move halfway across the country." His wife already worked for Brandon's company, so why not? He was in.

Brandon wanted to launch before his employee thought they were anywhere close to ready, though. Discussing the merits, he said "Perfection means you never took off; your plane is on the ground. We've got a plane. It's got one wing, one engine, no wheels, monkeys are flying it, and everything is just on fire. But as time goes on we're gonna add another wing and then an engine and then add a real pilot." They launched.

The following conversation took place with one of the biggest realtors in his area, just after his interview:

Realtor: "You do all this for free. When are you going to ask me for your business?"

Brandon: "I don't have to."

Realtor: "What do you mean?"

Brandon: "You just brought it up."

Realtor: "Oh, right."

Brandon ended up building something that separated his insurance company from the pack by leading with the give mentality. If he had waited until it was perfect, that plane would still be on the ground. One wing, one engine, no wheels, monkeys as pilots, and flames everywhere got him just where he wanted to go.

> **LESSON:** Nothing can ever be perfect, so just launch and iterate until you know if it'll work or not. If it doesn't you can move to the next thing before your competitors have even started.
>
> **BONUS LESSON:** You can only interview so many lenders and realtors before you start getting the same answers. That's what led Brandon to his next adventure back in Chapter 7.

Fuel growth through strategic 3-way wins

Strong strategic partnerships can expand your universe in ways you never dreamed possible if done correctly. Like the adage 1+1 is more than 2, leveraging relationships with others can mean the difference between average and life-changing results.

As you read in Chapter 10, Honorée Corder had written zero books in 2004 and is now a Strategic Book Coach who's published more than 50 books. Just writing that first book changed the trajectory of her career and life.

In 2016, Amazon invited her to speak about their publishing platform, KDP, at a media breakfast. They wanted to encourage more professionals to write and publish books on Amazon. In promoting the breakfast, they were going to feature her most recent book, which happened to be for divorced women. Since she's not a divorce expert and that's not what her work is about, though, it wouldn't have done much to help her career-wise.

It just so happened that the breakfast had to be rescheduled, opening a window of opportunity for her. She asked Amazon, "Would it be helpful if at least one of us had a book on why everyone should write and publish a book?" Of course they loved the idea because it would directly help them market their publishing service!

Honorée wrote *You Must Write a Book* and a companion workbook, *I Must Write My Book*. Since Amazon was behind the book and lots of people want to write books, she now also teaches a course on it and actually guides the process for some people. That one book has gotten her in Forbes, Fortune, and many other publications, as well as too many podcasts to count.

Her book created a 3-way win: Amazon can use it to promote their services, she earns royalties and lands new clients, and all of the readers learn valuable information that enables them to write their own book. This is a great example of how strategically helping others helps you.

None of the other speakers even thought to ask Amazon if writing a book would help. Honorée realized that featuring her most recent book about divorce wouldn't help her career, and had the foresight to come up with an idea that Amazon would want to promote because it would help promote their own service.

For Honorée, "It's the gift that keeps on giving" and now she gets "book babies," the books that people are inspired to write because of that book. "I get to be the person I wish I had when I first started."

She recommends that you market your book for both royalties and for new business. She says, "Give your best referral sources 25 books and let them give it to their best clients; then you have a 3-way win." The new business you gain can end up being much more profitable than the royalties from the book sales.

I use similar strategic partnerships with my last book, *Boomer Cashout: Increase Your Business's Value and Marketability to Sell for Retirement*. My work in economic development, advising Main Street Communities, and helping legacy businesses continue to operate prompted me to write the book. I was tired of trying to get business owners, especially boomers, to understand how critical it is that they use the web strategically if they ever want to have any chance of selling. Putting the advice in a book makes them take the advice more seriously.

A number of exit planners, business brokers, CPA's, and other professionals now give it to clients, which helps them save more small businesses. This is one of the things I'm most proud of because local businesses are part of the fabric of the community, part of people's lives, and places where memories are built. They even help attract other larger businesses to locate in the community, too.

So, take Honorée's advice and write a book! It can be one of the easiest ways to help many, many people.

> **LESSON:** Helping others get what they want can be key to unlocking great opportunities for yourself.

Chapter 14

Many people had to close their business because of COVID 19. Rachel had to start hers.

Working as a financial advisor, Rachel Garrett Mercer's business was built upon getting out in the community and building relationships. When the pandemic shutdown happened only essential workers were allowed to go to work, but she couldn't have gone even if she were allowed because she has Type 1 Diabetes, which put her at increased risk for severe illness.

She knew that even after the shutdown was loosened the health risk was just too great for her to work in the industry like she needed to. It was decision time, making her "reevaluate what my life was gonna be." How could she make a living? And how did she *want* to?

With a degree in stage management and a financial background, she realized she wanted to marry the idea of creativity with a client base. Recovering from carpal tunnel surgery, she "just decided, you know what? Life's too short not to start the thing that's just been pulling on my heart. I've had lots of pivots, lots of shifts, but now I feel like I'm in this space where I'm finally creating the thing that I was meant to."

Drawing on her background in and love for script development and storytelling, Rachel launched Mercer Editorial Services through which she offers copywriting, copy editing, content strategy, and social media management. Because of the type of work she does, she has the freedom of knowing that her career can't force her to be in a place that might put her health at risk.

Working from her mini-homestead farm in the middle of the worst pandemic in 100 years, Rachel has managed to build a booming business working with clients she likes, doing work she loves. Just several months after launching, though, she began to have friends contact her wanting to know how she started the business and how they might go about starting their own. She was unsure of how to proceed because she didn't feel qualified to advise them since she hadn't been in business long.

We had a coaching session and I told her, "Compared to them you're a veteran! You've been through the launch phase and are building a booming business. They've not even taken the first step but you have an active portfolio of real, live business clients who are paying you to deliver specific services." Then I shared with her the comment I related in Chapter 10, when Richard

Mulholland and his team were scrambling to create a new productized service because of COVID: "Nobody knows what they're doing. If everybody is a 2 out of 10 and we're a 3 out of 10, we're like kings!"

I think that's when Rachel began to realize she really is an entrepreneur, not a wantrepreneur.

LESSON: By finding a way to merge your personal interests with your experience and strengths, you can create a business that lets you live life like you want it.

Embrace your trauma to unleash your potential

Suffering from debilitating PTSD, anxiety, and depression resulting from sexual assault, a near-fatal car accident, and military-related incidents, retired and disabled Army veteran Annette Whittenberger began a blog called A Wild Ride Called Life as her own way of dealing with how she was feeling. Originally she never intended for it to be more than an online journal. "I needed an outlet to figure out what the heck was going on with me and to figure out that I wasn't alone."

"I lived so long hiding everything, from when I was a kid through the military and then afterwards. When you suppress all those feelings for so long you're just going to explode, and that's what happened to me. I exploded and I got into this really deep funk depression that, if I didn't find a way to spill it, I don't know how I would have made it through." A military wife and mother of two, she knew she needed to get better for her family as well.

After talking to a few of her former fellow soldiers and realizing they also had a difficult transition, she decided to use her blog as a platform for not only her own self-healing journey but to help others, too. She "wanted to show them I'm going through this and it sucks, but I can make it and so can you. It was terrifying because all those feelings that I was hiding inside were now out there for the world to see. It was like go big or go home, though."

Then she started getting messages from strangers thanking her for being so vulnerable. "I really cried the first time I saw one of those because you don't realize who's reading or watching or listening to your posts. You're kinda just making the posts as your own thing but you don't know who you affected just now with what you just said."

As she started surrounding herself with likeminded people, she "started getting the nerve to speak about it, to get on other people's podcasts and be a speaker, and it was just like *am I ready for this*?" Starting out as her personal journey and trying to help herself and other people, she wasn't planning on turning it into a business.

She slowly started realizing she wanted to make it into something bigger than just being a blogger, though.

Now Annette is on "a mission to erase the stigma of living with PTSD, anxiety and depression, and asking for help." She also started a podcast called The Truths We Hide where she talks with guests about their struggles and triumphs, to help listeners realize they aren't alone. Last year I was a guest on it, talking about the effects on my childhood and family after my grandfather killed himself when I was 5 and my grandmother tried to 3 years later. I had met Annette through my work with NASCAR driver Colin Garrett to combat veteran suicide, and we've bonded over wanting to help other families become healthier.

As a guest on my Adaptable Entrepreneurs live show, Annette said that "What helped me the most was having people who believed in me and who told me, 'you have a lot to offer, you have a story to tell.' That gave me a little bit more confidence to say *you know what, I can do this*. Every day, whether it's an off day or a good day, I still love what I do. I know there's someone out there I can talk to that can benefit." Her work to help others has now expanded through her debut book, *The Wall Between Two Lives: A True Story of Finding Purpose*.

LESSON: Being willing to share your own vulnerability can open doors to help yourself and others in ways you never dreamed of.

The one thing fear and faith have in common

Brian Bogert knows fear.

When he was 8 years old he went to a store with his mother and brother to get a 1" paint brush. A simple errand, but when he was walking back to their car a truck ran over him diagonally, tearing his spleen and completely severing his left arm from his body. The quick actions of a guardian angel nurse who just happened to be behind them saved his life and his arm, though it would take many years of painful physical therapy to regain full use of it.

So, yes, he knows fear, but Brian believes "The greatest things in life are on the other side of fear. So much of what keeps us stuck is ourselves, our lack of ability to see the bigger picture and understand options. We dismiss things without thought and attention. We can't see the path or we're too afraid of what it would look like, so we don't give ourselves permission to look at it."

If we really pay attention, though, we can learn from fear. He says that "Fear gives us feedback; most of the time we just don't pause to pay attention to the feedback. When we respond to emotion rather than feedback, we stay stuck."

To illustrate, Brian tells of taking his son mountain biking. After reaching the top, anxiety and fear took hold and his son was afraid to ride down. The thing is, though, when you're on top of a peak the only way out is down.

He worked with his son to "pick our line, see what obstacles we can identify. At some point, once we've mapped it out, we just have to let the brakes go and let it roll."

Brian recommends asking yourself these questions when you're afraid:

- Do you know the course you can chart and have you taken the time to pay attention to it?

- Do you know what obstacles might be in your way, ones you can see and anticipate and the ones you might not?

- Do you know the cliffs, the absolute things that will destroy?

- At what point do you move yourself from fear into faith?

Then, he says, it's time to "plot the course, understand the obstacles, understand the things that will kill, and let it roll. The only thing fear and faith have in common is an undetermined future."

LESSON: It's okay to be afraid, but paying attention to the feedback that fear gives is crucial to success.

The transformative effect of believing in yourself

Lynda Sunshine West grew up in a very volatile, abusive, alcoholic household, causing her to have a lot of fears and self-doubt which led to people pleasing behavior. Then, at age 51, while facing one fear every day for a year, she started an entrepreneurial and personal development journey that's totally transformed her life.

At the time she was working for a judge, "pushing paper all day." One day while driving to work, she thought, *this is so ridiculous, I don't understand this planet, I don't understand this life, why am I here?* Later that day she was in a private Facebook group and happened to see a plain text post by a woman she didn't know. It said that she's a life coach who took some time off and was now returning to her work. She was looking for five women who want to change their life. Lynda had no idea who she was but replied, "I'm in! I want to change my life."

That was the beginning of Lynda learning "who I am, what value I have to offer the planet, and what my purpose is here. In all the 51 years before that, I never even asked the question."

About 3 years into her journey, "Random people started calling me Sunshine, people I didn't know. About the fifth or sixth person later I thought, I need to look at this and see why they're calling me Sunshine? If they see something about me that is sunshine, that I bring light to people, then I'm going to embrace it and I'm gonna change my Facebook name to Lynda Sunshine West so I can embrace it on a regular, daily basis."

She says, "The embracing part of it was the hardest part." She'd been with her husband for 32 years and for all that time he had told her "how amazing and brilliant I am, but I didn't hear him because I wasn't ready to hear it. There's a saying that when the student is ready to learn the teacher will appear. The reality is the teacher is already there, the student just isn't ready yet. I wasn't ready until I was 51 to believe in myself."

When Lynda discovered her voice and her value she says she "made a declaration to myself: from this point forward I will share my voice every opportunity I get."

Her life is dramatically different now. She speaks on stages, interviews stars on the red carpet, makes TV and podcast appearances, and produces the Women Action Takers™ events. She's produced more than 100 events with up to 3,500 people in attendance, and has raised over $200,000 for charity.

Now she declares that her mission is to help 5 million women entrepreneurs share their voice with the world through her mastermind, collaboration projects, podcast, summits, live show, magazine, and events.

LESSON: Fear and self-doubt can make believing in yourself feel impossible, but once you truly believe in your own value and know what you have to offer the world you'll begin to recognize boundless opportunities that surround you.

What are you waiting for?

I can already hear you... "Some day I'll do this. Next year I'll do that. In 5 years I'll do this other thing." Blablabla. There's no time like now if you're serious about making changes, though!

Why would you wait? Is there a legitimate reason or are you just afraid? Before you know it next week turns into next month, turns into next year, and eventually turns into never. Regardless of the underlying reasons, it's just human nature to maintain the status quo because we tend to take the path of least resistance. But, face it, you're never going to have the life you want if you do that.

Mike "C-Roc" Ciorrocco, founder of People Building, Inc. and author of *Rocket Fuel*, is a fervent believer in not giving in to procrastination. He says, "Time is the fuel for fear. When you add time to something, fear grows if it's causing you to stop something. Not doing it right away is fueling the problem that's causing you to not get there."

He also points out that taking responsibility gives you

far greater control over your results. "Not taking responsibility leads to lack of control and chaos ensues; you end up feeling stuck and confused and start to blame others."

This kicks off a vicious cycle, one you can't get out of without actually acting because "lack of responsibility leads to waiting and procrastination, which leads to stress and confusion, which leads to more procrastination," C-Roc states. "You can end up feeling totally overwhelmed but you've done nothing to prevent that."

That doesn't mean he's perfect, though. C-Roc says he always feels like he's not doing enough and has to figure out a way to get unstuck every day. My guess is his own version of needing to get unstuck is nowhere near how much you need to get unstuck, but that's irrelevant.

I can tell you my own personal experience is that he's right about time being the fuel for fear. The time I spend worrying about doing something or obsessing about how to handle it is almost always worse than actually doing it once I get started. After I do it there's usually such a sense of accomplishment I wonder why I put it off in the first place and vow to never procrastinate again. Until the next time I do...

LESSON: It's easy to wait and hard to get started, but the longer you wait the more paralyzing your fear can become.

Chapter 15

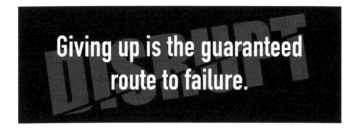

How many no's could you hear before you give up? What if the next one is your YES?

When Justin Breen was still employed as a senior editor, his company announced that his salary was being cut in half. There was no way he could meet his family's needs in the expensive city of Chicago on that income but he couldn't find a job and knew he had to do something drastic.

With zero business background, not even knowing what an LLC was, Justin started BrEpic Communications while still working at his half-salary job. He had a large network from his years as a journalist, probably 35,000 to 37,000 contacts, and started working his way through it.

Take a minute and try to guess how many no's he had to endure before he got his first 5 clients…

Go ahead, think about it and take a wild guess....

Justin actually reached out to 5,000 people to get his first 5 clients!

That's a success rate of 1/10 of 1%.

The day after he signed his fifth client he resigned from his job. Can you even imagine how satisfying that felt?

A couple of days later the top media columnist in the midwest, Robert Feder, wrote a story about him leaving the firm. Almost four months had passed since his salary cut was announced but those thousands of no's didn't make Justin give up. Truthfully, that just wasn't an option.

It's now just several years later and he has built a global business working with the top ½ of 1% of entrepreneurs in the world. After talking with thousands of successful entrepreneurs, he says they all have at least 2 of the following traits and the most successful have all 4:

- bankruptcy or potential bankruptcy
- depression
- the highest levels of anxiety you can imagine
- likely traumatic experiences as a child

If you think the ultra-successful had it easy, that they're just lucky, you're wrong. They have problems just like the rest of us but they rise above them, and many of them succeed because of those problems, not in spite of them.

Just recently another entrepreneur told me that after 30 years he "was an overnight success." That about sums it up.

> **LESSON:** If you quit, you'll never know if the next person you pitch would have been your yes.

The sharks aren't always right

When Charlynda Scales, founder of Mutt's Sauce, eventually pitched on Shark Tank, she didn't receive an offer because she wasn't ready to leave active duty Air Force. The sharks didn't believe she could focus on the business if she was serving.

When she did leave active duty later, she entered Bob Evans Farms' "Heroes to CEOs" contest, and won a $25,000 grant for her business. It included a mentorship session with contest co-host Daymond John, one of the sharks on Shark Tank. Daymond was actually the shark she really identified with and when reading his story she had always thought, *if he can do this, I can do this*. Charlynda told me, "Look at how the world works!" and that she cried when he first called her.

Winning the contest turned into a flurry of news appearances for Charlynda and Mutt's Sauce and the product was picked up by Kroger Stores. In the midst of all the PR and glamour, though, people didn't realize that she had recently gone through a divorce and was living in a 1-bedroom apartment in DC with no furniture, sleeping on a Coleman cot.

"I would go to interviews and sit at $1,000-a-plate dinners and be in gowns that I'd taped the receipt down because I'm taking it back the next day. Getting my makeup done at a kiosk in the Pentagon City Mall. I'm just doing what I can because I can't stop, because I know that somebody is deriving motivation from just seeing me continue going. They don't know what I'm going through, but they're like, 'Hey, she's still in this thing!'"

"I got to a point where I said *I've gotta get brave enough to tell people what's really going on.* I carried the shame with it for a little bit" because while she was going through the divorce, she was on the cover of Military Spouse magazine. She begged the editor not to put her on the cover, saying "I'm a failure of a milspouse because I'm getting a divorce, I left my husband." That prompted this exchange:

Editor: "Are you an entrepreneur?"

Charlynda: "Yes."

Editor: "Did you ask your husband for permission to start the business?"

Charlynda: "No, I just did it."

Editor: "Do you need his permission now to continue in your company?"

Charlynda: "No, I don't."

Editor: "Are you defined by whatever you do for your husband?"

Charlynda: "No."

Editor: "Well, there are other women who are tired of being defined by what they do for their husbands! That's not to say that it's a bad thing to support him but you have your own personality, your own things. I just want to tell that side; will you let me use that to tell that to power them up? You were a military spouse; you did this."

I can relate to how she felt a little bit because, although my husband is retired Navy with 26 years of service, I was only with him the last 6 years of that. I didn't feel I was a "real Navy wife" because I never had the hard parts of being a milspouse, of living through deployments. I made that comment to my friend Stephanie Brown, founder of The Rosie Network, when we first met and she set me straight. I realized, *I did quit a job and move to another state because of his career, and we had both of our kids before he retired. I was a real Navy wife.*

I first met Charlynda through Stephanie and she's such

an inspiration to everyone who learns of her story or comes in contact with her. Amazing things are to come!

> **LESSON:** Don't let losing pitches or worrying about what others think of you hold you back from realizing your dreams. Get up and keep going.

Obliterating boundaries

Imagine someone who's a tech startup mentor, entrepreneur, inventor, and business accelerator. They're the founder of a company that uses psychology and artificial intelligence to produce explosive results for clients and they have six PhD's on staff. This person's client list includes Microsoft, IBM, and Pearson. They have helped more than 50 startups scale up or turn around from the brink of disaster, hold four patents in machine learning and AI, and have written two books.

What would you guess their background is? You can probably visualize the type of person you expect them to be: their age, gender, race, ethnicity, area they grew up in, and level of education. And my guess is you're 99.99% likely to be wrong.

Manuj Aggarwal grew up in a small village in India where there's very little opportunity for work or education. Now the founder of TetraNoodle in Canada, he started his career in India at the age of 15 where he worked in a factory 12 hours a day, 6 days a week for $2/day. He "somehow scraped together enough money for a computer course" that cost more than a year's salary and it changed his life.

The fact that he was very introverted made computer programming perfect for him because he "didn't have to interact with the machines at all." He loved that he "could say do this and the computers did it."

He also met his now wife at the school but their marriage wasn't approved of. He says, "Ultimately I had to run away from home with only a suitcase full of clothes." After getting married, he and his wife moved to Canada to start a new life. He was fired from his very first job within 3 months because he didn't know the culture and language.

"A total outsider from all points of view," Manuj says, "I had every disadvantage but I can't do anything about my accent or skin color. This is what I have to work with, so let's focus on what I can do about it."

He asked himself, "What are the qualities I can hone that become so valuable that all other factors which are drawbacks for me become negligible? I have to live with this accent. I have to live with all these situations. But what else can I do which becomes so valuable to others that none of this matters any more?"

He and his staff at TetraNoodle "look at solutions that people generally don't look for. We look for solutions in different industries and apply them in a cross-pollinated manner. We look at the end result that anyone is trying to achieve and come up with the shortest and quickest path to that end goal."

The next time you're feeling sorry for yourself, feeling like things aren't fair and they're stacked against you, think of Manuj. If he can go from $2 a day to the boardrooms of Fortune 500 companies surely you can figure out a way to move forward.

> **LESSON:** Everyone has hurdles they have to overcome. Focus on the ones you can actually do something about and put aside the ones you can't.

"If I can close Netflix on my own, why do I need to work for someone else?"

About a year after Kerry Edelstein started Research Narrative, she was recruited for a sweet job at a large company where she would have run their custom market research practice in Los Angeles. She would have had a swanky corner office with a view of the Hollywood sign, a number of employees, a large expense account, and lots of travel.

A year earlier she might have taken it, but at this point she had just closed Netflix as a client. She said she thought, *I can't walk away from this, I have to see where it goes. If I'm already working with top brands like Netflix on my own, why do I need to work for someone else?*

Kerry's "why" in starting her business was that she "wanted to be autonomous. I want to call my own shots, decide who I work with and under what terms I work with them."

While working at a previous job, her nephew's best friend, an 18 year-old Honors Student and Eagle Scout, died suddenly and unexpectedly from a rare virus. The first thing she wanted to do was "get on a plane and spend two weeks at my sister's house helping my family out, helping them mourn, buying groceries, cooking dinner, doing whatever they needed from me because they were so shocked and crippled with grief. This was such a close family friend. But I had just started a new job where I had maybe a day of vacation built up, and no flexibility to work remotely. So I couldn't go. And even though they didn't fault me for it, it really tore me up inside to not be there for my family."

She says she never wanted to be in that position again, where she had to prioritize work over family without the discretion to choose, and vowed that "my next move is that I get to make that decision, not somebody else making that decision for me."

Now she finally had that autonomy and her dream client.

She puts it very succinctly: "A window office isn't worth it. I have a beautiful bay window in my home office."

> **LESSON:** When you truly understand why you're an entrepreneur, it makes it easier to keep competing decisions in perspective.

"No" isn't forever

Gable Eaton is a Marine veteran and the inventor of UTouch, a patented product you wear on your finger to provide protection from germs when interacting with public touchscreens or keypads. When asked how he came up with the idea, he said, "I did not like how my co-workers would touch my computer screen and leave those nasty fingerprints, smudges and germs behind, and I wanted a way to prevent it. UTouch popped into my head so I drew it and took it to an artist friend for a better rendition, then used that to get my patent."

The silicone product slides on your finger similar to a thimble, has a slot opening on the end for longer fingernails to fit through, and comes in a case that hangs conveniently on your keychain. The keychain case is also brandable, providing another target market as a promotional product.

Gable spent years developing the product and getting it patented, investing his own savings. Working full-time at other companies, though, he didn't have the resources to get the company off the ground and wasn't able to get a business loan. Time after time he was turned down but after relocating from Seattle to Chattanooga in 2017 to work for another company, he was making a delivery to the incubator CoLab when he heard about Bunker Labs.

Once he learned about the services Bunker Labs offers veteran entrepreneurs, he applied to and was accepted in their Veterans in Residence program, a six-month startup incubator. Gable says that program is what made the difference in helping him get all of his financials and plans in order.

Bunker Labs then connected him with Pathway Lending, a Community Development Financial Institution "that increases access to capital for underserved businesses in Tennessee and Alabama." Pathway provided the capital that enabled Gable to finally launch the company he had put so many years into.

Due to Gable's dogged persistence, TeqTouch is up and running successfully and he'll soon be launching his next product, OneTouch. Renee Bobb, a mentor with Bunker Labs was instrumental in him being selected to participate in the prestigious The Workshop at Macy's, the exclusive retail-vendor development program for diversity, along with Monifa Caines whom you met in Chapter 11.

Blake Hogan, CEO of Bunker Labs, told me that they knew Gable's product had promise and "lucky enough for Bunker, we had some folks at Pathway Lending who could help. Because of them, now he's got the space and the runway to succeed."

> **LESSON:** Rather than give up if you're having a hard time getting capital through the average bank, find the right support network who can help vet your idea, get your plan in order, and connect you to people who are more likely to be able to help.

"There has to be a reason I'm still here"

Basketball was Anita "AC" Clinton's life. Playing with a full scholarship at University of Illinois, her dream was to play professionally. In the second Big Ten Conference game of her Junior year, though, her dream evaporated when she "ripped everything in the knee to shreds. I knew immediately that my dreams, my hopes, my aspirations of playing professionally had just died."

"Basketball was my life. It was my everything. My entire persona, my entire identity, was wrapped inside the sport," AC said. "Once that was no longer an option for me, I had no clue who I was and what I was gonna do in the world." She decided life was no longer worth living, took all the pills prescribed post-surgery, went to sleep intending to never wake again. "However, about 4 hours later I woke up and every pill came back up. In the hospital I heard the doctor say, 'It's truly a miracle that she's still alive.' "

"From that point my question became *why am I still here*? I wanted to know my purpose, my reason for existence. I knew this was not an accident. There has to be a reason that I'm still here. What is that reason?" That began her twenty-year journey to find the answer.

A pivotal moment came one afternoon as she was fighting rush hour traffic. "I'm behind an 18-wheeler that starts to slow down; there's nothing in front of him and I'm thinking *what is he doing*. As he starts to pull over, I drive past and look in my rear view mirror, seeing that what caught his attention was a lady, a prostitute, walking down the street. I pulled over about ½ block away and continued looking at her in the rear view mirror. If you could see her look, it was very clear she wasn't happy and I kinda imagine what the conversation was when she got in the truck. In that moment the tears started streaming down my eyes."

AC thinks of the woman as "Trina" and told me, "I wanted to run to her and say *Trina, there is something on this earth that you are called to do and this isn't it*. At that point I had nothing to offer her, though. I could give her a couple of dollars but how long was that gonna last her? From that point I was like *okay, I've gotta figure out how I can help women and men like Trina who are working jobs that they absolutely hate, that they don't enjoy, that they're not passionate about. What can I do to help them figure out what it is that they're purposed to do?* Trina, for me, was the thing that was irking me and forced me to create Be Great."

After all those years of searching for her purpose, she founded the company Be Great Global to help others figure out their own purpose. AC refers to what she calls your "genius box." When you can figure out what you're passionate about and what you have the skill or talent to do, you find your genius box.

"Passion plus genius, how do those two benefit other people or other things? If you can find that sweet spot, now you're closer to knowing what it is you were created to do. Another variable is what's a pain, challenge or problem in the world that irks you? It just bothers the heck out of you. Most of the time that is the thing that you are the answer to. The world needs all of what we all have to offer. Can you imagine if 50% of the population would step into the thing that they've been created to do?"

She recommends that you go through your passions one by one, listing things you enjoy and might want to pursue. "It's not enough to be gifted at something, though; you need to enjoy it once you get into it. And there's always pushback because, for most people, the thing you're purposed to do is so much bigger than you. You can't even imagine that. *What, I can do that?* We start small, start taking small steps and we test out things."

AC finds that practicing affirmations is a great help with mindset. "I have them write an affirmation, all positive words, and read it back. The more you say it the more you believe it. In most instances it becomes reality. I believe we create our own reality." And she's living proof of that.

> **LESSON:** Even if you're ready to quit on yourself, the world needs the unique skills and experience that only you have! There are people you can help that you haven't even met yet.

PART FIVE - Higher Purpose

Chapter 16

If you're extracting or abusing the value of everybody around you, that's just not sustainable.

Daryl Hatton's underlying secret is helping others and his first principle is "to start with being generous, give away trust. Our little team of 10 in Vancouver, Canada, has helped raise almost $200,000,000 for over 200,000 projects in over 40 countries around the world."

Of course they need to make money to continue to operate, but their business model gives the fundraising service for free to the charities, and supporters are happy to tip them so the platform can continue to be available for the charities. Everyone wins.

Daryl says, "We're having a pretty big impact on how much good we can create in the world out of what we do, but I didn't set out to change the world." Personally, I think his generous nature enabled him to see the opportunity, though. Somebody else would still be hunting for a way to make a dime off of everyone.

"You can win big, you can win big time, but at the end of your life you just don't have that well-populated of a funeral. Nobody wants to show up because they gave it to you their whole life." Well said, Daryl.

> **LESSON:** Being loved for the good you do will outlast any admiration there is for the money you have.

Helping others helps your bottom line

In her work as Executive Director of Kevin Bacon's Six Degrees, Stacy Huston continually sees that companies can actually see an ROI when they help others. It's something that builds value and participation in their employees.

Stacy says employees are "actually more actively engaged in their day-to-day job because they have higher job satisfaction, and that's just factual, data-driven stats. When you give your employees 8 hours a month or quarter to donate their time, or you have organized activities where they're giving back, there's a direct correlation to increasing your bottom line at a company."

Samples is the number 4 staffing agency in Colorado but their specific area of expertise is helping those who are differently abled get gainful employment. The founders led by example by employing many people in their restaurant through the staffing agency. Stacy said they found "it created an environment with so much more empathy and enjoyment and people started to work not so focused on themselves. It allows people to work on a lot of different things that they wouldn't typically be able to," and staff who were able to help the differently abled employees felt more fulfilled.

When The Bacon Brothers were going to be in Colorado for a concert, Six Degrees arranged for them to visit the restaurant for lunch, meet with employees and customers, and do a popup concert to help raise awareness of the work Samples is doing.

Six Degrees allows celebrities to get as much enjoyment as the people they interact with. According to Stacy, the events they organize are "really fun and a low lift, and celebrities who don't typically get to do this kind of stuff get an interesting, unique opportunity to do a lot of good by spending an hour or two of their day when they're otherwise going to be in a trailer waiting for a stage call. A small amount of time gives lasting value. There's an energy about these events that I can't really describe but they're so fun, and the joy it brings to so many people. To have just a little part of that is so special."

LESSON: When you focus on helping others rather than just on making money, you often receive more than you give.

"I have the whole prison system on my back"

Fifteen years in prison would break many people but Shawn Barksdale took control of his life within those walls. Now an entrepreneur, he is also dedicated to helping create a better community. Shawn told me, "I was one of the people who helped destroy the community, so it's only right that I and others like me help mend it."

He mentors youth in the community and speaks at schools, including those for special needs. Shawn's charisma makes it easy for him to connect, and an autistic child at one of the schools has stayed in touch with him. The child even called one day to tell Shawn that he had learned how to code and had created a website.

He encourages other young people to find an outlet for their anger, like working out or boxing, so they "put the guns down" and don't end up incarcerated like he was. Since they know where he's been, he can talk straight with them. It's very different from a parent or teacher saying it.

It doesn't stop with kids, though. Shawn mentors others who are incarcerated or have been released, to help them learn entrepreneurial skills and reintegrate into society in a productive way. "I chose to change how the world viewed me," and he wants to help others do the same.

It's important that they believe in themselves so others can believe in them, and Shawn helps them do that. He told me, "We're not only staying out of trouble, we're showing we can run the community."

Because of his success, there's even more pressure for him to continue to succeed. People who work within the prison system as well as those who are incarcerated have said, "If Shawn can't do it, nobody can." He said, "I feel like I have the whole prison system on my back," but I know his back is strong.

LESSON: Your past mistakes don't disqualify you from helping others. If anything, they make you even more qualified to do so.

"It's not my money"

Faith is the centerpiece of everything Stacey Burns-Fox does. She said, "I truly believe that God has given me the gifts and resources he's given me to be a good steward and to use those. It's not my money, but it's money He's given me to use while I'm here on this earth. So when I am presented with a great cause I have to figure out a way to help fund it."

One of the things she does is partner with an organization that encourages women to start their own businesses in impoverished countries. For example, in

2019 she donated over 250 bridal gowns for women in Peru to start businesses that sell and rent them out. Stacey says, "They time out of the orphanage at 18 and if they don't have a job they generally go into prostitution if they're not married. We're teaching women how to be entrepreneurs and to have a job and have an income. Plus, there aren't a lot of pretty wedding dresses there to get married. The sanctity of that institution is so important to me, that if they can get married and feel a part of that unit then they'll never be on the street. That's really nice and important to me."

Stacey is also the co-founder of Bras For the Cause, a nonprofit committed to strengthening Iowa communities by educating and encouraging the importance of early detection of breast and cervical cancers. The charity holds unique fundraisers like auctioning off decorated bras and other items to raise money to pay for free breast and cervical screenings.

Working with the Princess Project and Project Prom, she gives a free dress to anyone who needs it. "I never want somebody not to go to prom because they didn't have the outfit to wear. I think it's the second most important dress you'll wear in your life, the first being your wedding dress. I just am very fortunate that I get to be a part of women's lives for the two most important days of their lives." She's also been known to give the most expensive prom dress in her shop to a special needs teen.

Stacey's mantra is "faith over fear," which helps her live with the attitude of *what's the worst that can happen* in everything she does.

> **LESSON:** Often the person volunteering or donating gets back more than they give.

Disruptive Philanthropy

Most people just think of donations or volunteering when they think of philanthropy, but Ryan Garrett and I think that's the least effective way of reaching transformative goals. We know that strategic collaboration can help nonprofits and businesses do amazing things together.

Ryan's son, 21-year-old Colin Garrett, is a NASCAR Xfinity Series driver. While other teams are going after the same large companies' advertising dollars, we're approaching it as more of a B2B service that combines social responsibility and delivers a real ROI to companies that partner with us. We've worked on things like helping place veteran owned products in retail chains, promoting franchise opportunities to veterans, and helping recruit, hire, and retain veteran employees.

Right after I started working on strategy with Colin and Ryan in late 2018, the nonprofit Racing For Heroes wanted help developing a national awareness campaign. Their mission is to combat veteran suicide by providing free mental and physical health services, job training and placement, and motorsports therapy. It struck me personally since my husband is retired military and my family has a history of suicide.

Money spent on a national awareness campaign would have taken funds directly from treatments, though, and a national awareness campaign is worthless without a national platform. Since both of Colin's brothers are active duty, supporting the military is personal for the Garretts. They agreed to roll Racing For Heroes into the work we were doing together and we've been promoting them pro bono ever since. In November 2019 we added The Rosie Network to the mix; that's a nonprofit founded by military spouse Stephanie Brown to provide free entrepreneur training and mentoring.

Originally we just planned to have the logos on the car but the idea kept growing. As Ryan says, "We went from being able to picture this a little bit to *wait a minute, maybe it could be this*. The vision kept expanding. This tiny little idea kept becoming more detailed and getting richer. The further we went, the more meaningful we saw it could become."

Our holistic strategy promotes causes important to the military community, small businesses owned by veterans and military spouses, and companies that support the military community. Since the military is a true cross-section of America, anything we do to help them ripples out to help others.

Colin's disruptive campaign to combat veteran suicide has already made NASCAR history. Just a few examples include:

- first crowdfunded Xfinity Series car
- first to pay for stem cell treatments for a veteran with MS
- first to let micro businesses be part of a national campaign
- first Black-owned, Service Disabled Veteran-owned NASCAR sponsor: Body Aqua

We're now partnering with the first blind-owned sponsor that we're aware of, Hoby's Collective, owned by PhD chemist Hoby Wedler. The partnership will promote awareness of the need for accessibility for everyone, not just the blind, and we'll be crowdfunding to help pay for the tooling for Hoby's seasonings to have Braille labels.

We want to help other companies grasp the fact that 26% of adults in the US have some kind of disability. Dismissing 1 of every 4 potential customers just isn't good business, whether in person or on your website!

Ryan is a semi-retired partner in a large financial services firm and says, "After accomplishing the things I wanted to do in my day job, I have this whole new passion. I found I needed something that I wasn't sure would work again. When things are successful and going well it's great and fun but finding something again that might not work, topped off by all the good we can do, is thrilling. The passion and things that excite me about this adventure have nothing to do with racing. I've learned to love racing but that's not what's driving me. What's driving me is the adventure and the possibilities of the difference we can make."

LESSON: Philanthropy doesn't have to be limited to donations and volunteering. Campaigns can serve a greater good and realize an ROI at the same time. The possibilities are endless!

PART ONE: Getting "You" Right

Chapter 1:
It's your business and you can make it anything you want.

1. Remembering your dreams is the beginning of reimagining your business to reinvent your life.

2. If you're too proud to be honest with yourself, you may as well stop reading now.

3. Pay attention to what other people are suggesting you do. They often see things in you and recognize opportunities that you don't.

4. Now is the time to decide the things that are most important to you and what you're willing to change to get them.

5. Small changes can add up to truly living your life by design.

6. Figure out a way to encourage yourself to do something every day, even if it seems tiny, to help you reach your goals.

7. Concentrate on what you can control rather than

worry about what you can't control.

Chapter 2:
If a blind man can grow the grass, you can do this.

8. Stop using convenient excuses for not doing the things you're capable of; free your mind and the rest will follow.

9. Pay attention to what you liked as a child; it may just hold the secret to your success and fulfillment as an adult.

10. Make it a habit to consciously look for a positive way to look at anything negative. There's always a flipside.

11. Mindset is everything.

12. Every problem creates an opportunity; flip the excuses for why you can't succeed into reasons that you must.

13. Your toughest challenges can provide breakthroughs that change your life.

14. Conventional wisdom isn't set in stone. You can prove it wrong with the right work ethic and preparing yourself for opportunities that may arise.

Chapter 3:
What's your victory condition?

15. If you don't know where you're going, you won't know when you get there.

16. It can be much easier to know what you don't want than what you want, so start there in envisioning your life.

17. Even if you don't want something, it might just be because you haven't seen it in a form you would like yet.

18. It's imperative that you understand what best meets your overall goals: building a lifestyle business or one that's focused primarily on growth.

19. Understand what you really want out of the business, where your passions lie, and what you'll need to give up to grow. Then, analyze whether your next step is truly worth it to you in terms of time, money, and stress.

20. Understand what's important to you and live your life using that as a guidepost.

21. Focusing more inward can help you make better choices and feel more fulfilled in the long run.

22. By concentrating your strengths where they're needed and being vigilant about protecting your time, you can successfully manage multiple roles.

23. Don't worry about making huge changes all at once. Making a slight nudge is much less scary, lets you test the waters, and can produce surprising results.

24. We can't say it too many times: build a business

that helps you reach your own personal goals and your own definition of success. Otherwise, you may as well get a job. At least you can just walk away from that if you get sick of it.

Chapter 4:
There's only one YOU.

25. There are companies who need what only you can bring and people whose lives can be changed by learning from you. Stop discounting your value.

26. Skills and talents are portable across industries; the possibilities are limitless.

27. Sometimes the things you do get noticed; be ready to leverage that.

28. It's time to honor yourself and the way you're made.

29. Identify what's perceived as your greatest shortcomings to help uncover your greatest strengths.

30. Honoring your strengths and the things you enjoy provides the foundation for you to stand out from the competition.

31. We can turn challenges in our lives into assets that make us stronger.

PART TWO: Expanding Your Network & Mind

Chapter 5:
Get in the right sandbox.

32. Take the time now to figure out the sandbox you're really meant to be in, where you can work with people you sincerely enjoy, use your skills to make the most impact, and experience business in a way that will be the most personally fulfilling to you.

33. Don't let career decisions you made at a very young age lock you in and prevent you from even exploring other possibilities. Part of education is about keeping an open mind.

34. High revenues are meaningless if it's all flowing back out the door for overhead. Check your ego, clean house, and shatter your own glass ceiling.

35. Knowing your own canary in the coal mine gives you the ability to head off problems early and make changes that may be needed for you to be more fulfilled in the business.

36. You can never go wrong by checking to see if your own attitude is part of the problem.

37. Choose your clients wisely and remember you always have the right to say no.

Chapter 6:
Create your own luck.

38. You create your own luck by constantly seeking

out opportunity and being ready to seize it when you find it.

39. Keep your eyes open because you never know when an opportunity might arise, even if you don't recognize it.

40. You don't have to have your life's journey completely mapped out to be successful and fulfilled. It's a unique tapestry that you can create as you go.

41. Prioritize what's important to you and build your business around that rather than building your life around your business.

42. Look for opportunities to make others smarter and don't be afraid to reach out to important companies or people.

Chapter 7:
"The best thing I ever did was go to Elaine's."

43. When you know what you want to achieve and the types of people you need to meet to make the right connections, you can put yourself in a strategic position to meet them.

44. Don't just interview potential employees. Also interview those who will provide the professional support you need to succeed, and make sure they truly understand you and your strengths and goals.

45. Just being around people who are more

successful than you helps challenge your thought patterns and can truly push you to new heights.

46. Investing in yourself by working with the right coaches and masterminds can be the best investment you'll ever make, with an ROI that greatly exceeds anything.

47. The right professional advice can help transform your business. Don't assume it's only for the big guys.

Chapter 8:
To get the right answers you have to ask the right questions.

48. The devil is in the details. Find a trusted advisor who knows the right questions to ask so you can get the right answers.

49. There's way more to starting a business than how much money you can make.

50. Knowing who wants what you have makes it easier to create multiple revenue streams from products and services they really want.

51. Make a conscious effort every day to recognize that you have choices, that things don't have to stay the way they are. Then make smart choices that let you make small tweaks that add up to big change.

52. Having experience in a field isn't critical for

becoming successful in it. Self-motivation, determination, and willingness and ability to learn are, though.

53. To attract great clients and command higher prices, you must become an expert in your field AND define what you want to do, who you want to do it for, what you don't want to do, and who you don't want to do it for.

PART THREE: Thinking & Creating

Chapter 9:
Focus on the customer's pain.

54. Try to solve the customer's pain rather than trying to make them understand your product.

55. You can always learn from people who aren't experts in your field, and they can learn from you. Just a different perspective can often make 1+1 equal more than 2.

56. People love to be different or feel like they know or have something that others don't. Adding an air of scarcity, exclusivity, or limited availability to your marketing can work wonders.

57. Practice being curious: include the questions of why, why not, and what if on a regular basis to start seeing past what's obvious.

58. You can win the race to zero if you find someone else to pay for the product or service you're providing.

59. Look for areas where others have become complacent; they're ripe for disruption because everyone else is lazy or entrenched in legacy thinking.

60. Ideas are one of the most valuable things on earth; learn to view yours as such.

Chapter 10:
"No, bro, we just read the email you got."

61. You can make a shit ton of money by knowing a shit ton about one thing that others are too lazy or busy to bother with.

62. Sometimes you need to adjust your route to achieve the level of success you want. Specializing is one way to do that: you'll end up with less competition, will stand out more, and can become the go-to expert.

63. Finding the sweet spot where you can deliver the most value to your clients and get the most value yourself is key to developing a profitable niche.

64. To truly differentiate yourself from competitors, write a well thought-out, professional book.

65. Being authentic in a way that turns off people you don't want to work with actually helps attract people you do want to work with because they recognize you as "one of them."

Chapter 11:
Identifying the dragon

66. I can't say it better than Rich: "If they say yes and give you the money, you know you've identified the dragon."

67. You don't always have to create a new product; you can adapt existing products to meet a challenge or give them your own unique twist.

68. People all around you are having fun doing things that could be turned into new business ideas.

69. If someone else controls your customers, they control your business and future.

70. Your future might just lie in solving a problem that's personally important to you.

71. Take time to research and ease into doing something new rather than jumping in all at once. You'll be more prepared if you decide to go with it, but will also be saved from making a bad decision if you find it's not for you.

72. Asking a lot of questions up front and doing quick and dirty iterations to get customer feedback is the best way to decide if an idea is even worth pursuing.

PART FOUR: Starting & Doing

Chapter 12:
Focus your efforts on things that support your long term goals.

73. Following through on a daily plan that focuses your efforts and supports your long term goals gives you more control over reaching those goals successfully.

74. Working on the business instead of in the business gives you much more freedom and lets you build a more valuable business that you may someday be able to sell.

75. Relying on other businesses too much for the operation of your own lets them control your future.

76. Figure out the two or three things that you're best at and enjoy the most, delegate everything else, and only work with the clients who are a good fit for you.

77. When you can envision what you want, you can reverse engineer to understand what you need to do to get there and when you need to do it.

78. It's important to create processes that work for you, but don't try to do everything at once.

Chapter 13:
Get off your big BUT.

79. Opportunity surrounds you, but it's up to you to

get off your big BUT and take action to seize it. Nobody is going to chase you down and beg you to act.

80. Learn to tune out advice from the middle-of-the-bell-curve people without vision who can't understand why you don't just play it safe.

81. Sometimes dreams really are trying to send you a message.

82. Diversifying gives you more tools to withstand volatility and meeting challenges head-on gives you an invaluable opportunity to learn and grow.

83. Even Kool Kel was depressed when the pandemic hit. Now you can stop feeling guilty.

84. Nothing can ever be perfect, so just launch and iterate until you know if it'll work or not. If it doesn't you can move to the next thing before your competitors have even started.

85. You can only interview so many lenders and realtors before you start getting the same answers.

86. Helping others get what they want can be key to unlocking great opportunities for yourself.

Chapter 14:
What's the worst that could happen?

87. By finding a way to merge your personal interests with your experience and strengths, you can create a business that lets you live life like

you want it.

88. Being willing to share your own vulnerability can open doors to help yourself and others in ways you never dreamed of.

89. It's okay to be afraid, but paying attention to the feedback that fear gives is crucial to success.

90. Fear and self-doubt can make believing in yourself feel impossible, but once you truly believe in your own value and know what you have to offer the world you'll begin to recognize boundless opportunities that surround you.

91. It's easy to wait and hard to get started, but the longer you wait the more paralyzing your fear can become.

Chapter 15:
Giving up is the guaranteed route to failure.

92. If you quit, you'll never know if the next person you pitch would have been your yes.

93. Don't let losing pitches or worrying about what others think of you hold you back from realizing your dreams. Get up and keep going.

94. Everyone has hurdles they have to overcome. Focus on the ones you can actually do something about and put aside the ones you can't.

95. When you truly understand why you're an entrepreneur, it makes it easier to keep

competing decisions in perspective.

96. Rather than give up if you're having a hard time getting capital through the average bank, find the right support network who can help vet your idea, get your plan in order, and connect you to people who are more likely to be able to help.

97. Even if you're ready to quit on yourself, the world needs the unique skills and experience that only you have! There are people you can help that you haven't even met yet.

PART FIVE: Higher Purpose

Chapter 16:
How many people will be at your funeral?

98. Being loved for the good you do will outlast any admiration there is for the money you have.

99. When you focus on helping others rather than just on making money, you often receive more than you give.

100. Your past mistakes don't disqualify you from helping others. If anything, they make you even more qualified to do so.

101. Often the person volunteering or donating gets back more than they give.

102. Philanthropy doesn't have to be limited to donations and volunteering. Campaigns can serve a greater good and realize an ROI at the same time. The possibilities are endless!

Afterword by Charles Kipps

When Lisa Kipps-Brown decided to write *Disrupt Your Now*, she called me and asked if I wanted to co-write the book with her. It made sense. She is the technical adviser for my website as well as the source of extremely valuable business counsel. I am the author of eight books and had ghost written three. But there was another connection.

Lisa is my cousin.

Long before either of us imagined where we would be at this point, we saw each other at various get togethers. During one of those gatherings my Uncle Glenn, Lisa's father, played pitch and catch with me. What made that unusual? Uncle Glenn was blind. In fact, he was a great inspiration for me and my entire family in that, as Lisa points out in the book, he never made excuses for his blindness. My younger brother is named Glenn in his honor.

In preparation for our writing the book, Lisa and I interviewed a number of successful entrepreneurs who offer advice within the pages. It was incredibly enlightening. After the interviews were complete, Lisa sent me a few sample pages.

Well, those pages were so well written, so personal, that I realized *Disrupt Your Now* could not be *our* book, it had to be *Lisa's* book.

What Lisa has done is quite extraordinary — harnessing the knowledge and experience of hugely successful people and distilling it into a guide like no other. So sit back and have yourself a wonderful read. And if you dare, *Disrupt Your Now*.

Charles Kipps
New York City
Award-winning Writer/Producer

Appendix: Meet the Entrepreneurs

in the order they first appear...

Steve Sims, founder of Sims Media, Bluefish, and author of the international bestseller *Bluefishing: The Art of Making Things Happen*

Manuel Astruc, MD, Psychiatrist turned Executive Coach

Richard Mulholland, founder of Missing Link, author of the books *Legacide*, *Boredom Slayer*, and *Story Seller*

B. Jeffrey Madoff, founder of Madoff Productions, author of *Creative Careers: Making a Living With Your Ideas,* playwright, theater producer

Tamara Linnan, founder of Profitable Shenanigans, veteran, hashtag queen

Shawn Barksdale, founder of Press For Time Tees and host of Ten Minutes of Truth podcast

Sande Golgart, President of Zonez

Sherman Williams, founder of Body Aqua functional beverages, veteran

Henry Sims, co-owner of Sims Media

Derek Hartley and Romaine Patterson, hosts of the award-winning radio show and podcast Derek & Romaine, founders of DNR Travel

Stacey Burns-Fox, founder of Stacey's Bridal, Prom, and Mastectomy Center

Stacy Huston, Executive Director of Kevin Bacon's Six

Degrees organization, co-founder of TEDxTysons, electrical vehicle infrastructure consultant

Dr. Hoby Wedler, blind PhD chemist, flavor scientist, founder of Hoby's

Brian Bogert, founder of Brian Bogert Companies. human behavior and performance coach

Adam White, author of *Motown: The Sound of Young America*, former Editor-in-Chief of Billboard magazine and retired Universal Music Group International's VP of Communications

Trevor Johnson, teenage entrepreneur who is on the autism spectrum

Aaron Golub, first legally blind person to play NCAA Division I football, keynote speaker, host of Blind Ambition podcast, financial investment advisor

Bernard Evans, celebrity hairstylist, holds a wide range of patents in the hair care industry, creator of K.A.S.H. entrepreneur training system

Daryl Hatton, crowdfunding visionary, founder of ConnectionPoint and its brands FundRazr, Sponsifi, and CoCoPay, keynote speaker

Kerry Edelstein, founder of Research Narrative

Charles Kipps, writer/producer; winner of Emmy, Peabody, Humanitas, and Edgar awards; author of nonfiction and fiction books including The Conor Bard Mysteries; Grammy-Nominated record producer with seven Gold Records

Justin Breen, founder of BrEpic Communications and

author of *Epic Business*

Brandon Straza, founder of The Success Finder, host of The Mastermind Effect podcast

Mark Milen, founder of Innovate Holdings procurement

Phyllis Pieri, CFE, franchise expert and *Your Franchise Coach*

Emily Mishler, founder of The Cultivated Group and author of the children's book series *Esmè the Curious Cat*

Catherine Tanner, CEO of 3P&T Security Recruiting

Marlana Semenza, strategic brand communicator, founder of Marlana Semenza Photography

Matthew Alex, founder of Beyond Academics

Kelvin Joseph, founder of Kool Kel Marketing

Honorée Corder, Strategic Book Coach, founder of Honorée Enterprises

Brooke Norman, founder of First6Media and author of *hey…you're muted: The Essential Post-COVID Marketing Handbook*

J. Roberto Inderbitzin, founder of REFRAME Design Studio, multi-disciplinary designer

Samanta Joseph, founder of Samanta Shoes

Monifa Caines, founder of Queen of Spades Style, veteran

Todd Connor, founder of Bunker Labs, author of *Third Shift Entrepreneur*, veteran

Blake Hogan, founder of BreakAway Safety Solutions, CEO of Bunker Labs, veteran

Tab Pierce, founder of founder of companies Caliber Security Partners and Refiners, author of *Upsurge: Wreckage to Triumph, Rebuilding Your Personal and Business Life*

Matt Deutschman, founder of Doubletake Promotional Marketing

Bill Bloom, founder of Bloom Financial and author of *Retire as You Desire*

Evan Guzman, founder of The MilBrand Project, former Global Head of Military Programs and Engagement for Verizon

Dr. Greg S. Reid, entrepreneur, film producer, keynote speaker, and award-winning author of numerous books including *Stickability: The Power of Perseverance* and *Three Feet From Gold*

Charlynda Scales, founder of Mutt's Sauce, Shark Tank competitor, veteran

Rachel Garrett Mercer, founder of Mercer Editorial Services

Annette Whittenberger, founder of A Wild Ride Called Life, host of The Truths We Hide podcast, author of *The Wall Between Two Lives: A True Story of Finding Purpose*, veteran

Lynda Sunshine West, Founder of Women Action Takers, Queen of Collaboration, Speaker, 6X Bestselling Author, Mastermind Facilitator, Executive Film

Producer, Red Carpet Interviewer

Mike "C-Roc" Ciorrocco, founder of People Building, Inc. and author of *Rocket Fuel*

Manuj Aggarwal, founder of TetraNoodle

Gable Eaton, inventor of Utouch and OneTouch, founder of TeqTouch, veteran

Anita "AC" Clinton, founder of Anita Clinton Enterprises and Be Great Global, host of the Be Great Global podcast

Ryan Garrett, disruptive philanthropist, Dad of NASCAR Xfinity Series driver Colin Garrett

About the Author

The author of *Boomer Cashout*, Lisa Kipps-Brown's natural talent for transforming basic ideas into disruptive strategy and valuable collaborations has people like Forbes 30 Under 30-listed blind PhD chemist Dr. Hoby Wedler calling her a "cognitive powerhouse." Steve Sims, author of *Bluefishing*, says she's a unicorn who bridges the gap between digital natives and digital immigrants, helping entrepreneurs solve big picture problems.

Since starting her web & marketing strategy company in 1996, Lisa has been a pioneer in business use of the web. Her achievements include saving companies from bankruptcy and tripling CARES Act money for rural communities. Take it from one of her clients: "if you're not afraid of challenging the status quo, Lisa Kipps-Brown can help you build a business that's sustainable and means more than money."

She's the expert you're missing, and likely didn't even know you need. No gobbledygook, guaranteed!

Find out more about her consulting services, live show, and speaking engagements at LisaKippsBrown.com.

Made in the USA
Columbia, SC
23 July 2021

42255620R00148